STREETCAR TO JUSTICE

STREETCAR  TO JUSTICE

How Elizabeth Jennings Won the Right to Ride in New York

by Amy Hill Hearth

GREENWILLOW BOOKS
An Imprint of HarperCollins*Publishers*

Streetcar to Justice: How Elizabeth Jennings Won the Right to Ride in New York
Text copyright © 2018 by Amy Hill Hearth
Jacket: Photograph of New York City streetcar, 1889, courtesy of New-York Historical Society;
painting of Elizabeth Jennings copyright © 2018 by Cozbi Cabrera;
undated photograph of Elizabeth Jennings courtesy of Kansas Historical Society
Page ii: illustration reprinted courtesy of the Museum of the City of New York

The text of this book is set in ITC Century.
Book design by Christy Hale

Library of Congress Control Number: 2017959047.

ISBN 978-0-06-267360-2 (trade ed.)

18 19 20 21 22 PC/LSCH 10 9 8 7 6 5 4 3 2 1
First Edition

Greenwillow Books

FOR

Lee H. Hill Jr.,
my father, who taught me to love history,
and for the Delany sisters,
from whom I learned history firsthand

Contents

Three Notes about Language   1

PART I: *A Day like No Other*   3

ONE: *"Those Monsters in Human Form"*   5

    THE FIRST NEW YORKERS   12

TWO: *Stray Dogs and Pickpockets*   15

    SLAVERY IN THE NORTH   22

    TIMELINE: THE END OF SLAVERY IN NORTHERN STATES   24

THREE: *A City Divided by Race*   27

    WHAT WAS JIM CROW?   31

FOUR: *"I Screamed Murder with All My Voice"*   35

FIVE: *"You Will Sweat for This!"*   37

SIX: *An Admired Family*   39

    FREDERICK DOUGLASS AND THE BLACK PRESS   44

    WHO SHOULD GO TO SCHOOL?   46

SEVEN: *A "Shameful" and "Loathsome" Issue*   49

    TRYING TO MAKE A DIFFERENCE   55

    WILLIAM LLOYD GARRISON AND *THE LIBERATOR*   56

    HORACE GREELEY AND THE *NEW YORK DAILY TRIBUNE*   57

EIGHT: *A Future U.S. President*   59

    THE FUGITIVE SLAVE ACT   60

    CHESTER A. ARTHUR: HIS EARLY YEARS   62

NINE: Elizabeth Jennings v. Third Avenue Railroad Company   65

    GETTING TO BROOKLYN   68

TEN: *The Jury's Decision*   71

PART II: *A Forgotten Hero*   77

ELEVEN: *An Uncanny Similarity to Rosa Parks*   79

TWELVE: *What Happened to Elizabeth Jennings?*   85

    THE CIVIL WAR DRAFT RIOTS   86

    THE FIRST FREE KINDERGARTEN FOR COLORED CHILDREN IN NEW YORK CITY   88

THIRTEEN: *How a Creepy Old House Led to the Writing of This Book*   91

FOURTEEN: *Retracing Her Footsteps*   95

POSTSCRIPT: *Chester A. Arthur: Tragedy Leads to Presidency*   101

Bibliography   105

Notes   113

Author's Note about Elizabeth Jennings's Age in 1854   121

Suggested Reading   123

Elizabeth Jennings's Life within a Historical Timeline   124

Important Locations   127

Acknowledgments   129

Illustrations   133

Index   137

About the Author   143

"I screamed murder with all my voice."

—Elizabeth Jennings, 1854

Three Notes about Language

LANGUAGE IS NEVER STAGNANT. The meaning and intent of words can change over time. That is the case with the word *colored*, which is not accepted today because it has evolved into a loaded word meant to be racist and hurtful.

Colored was once commonly used to refer to black or African American people. African Americans frequently used the word *colored* in Elizabeth Jennings's era. *The Colored American*, for example, was a black newspaper in New York founded in 1837. Other examples of the use of the word by the African American community include the First Colored Presbyterian Church and First Colored American Congregational Church, churches in New York City. Frederick Douglass used the term *colored* in his publications, several of which are quoted from in this book.

Readers may also note that the term *civil rights*, which is a common phrase describing the struggle for equality among races, has been replaced with *equal rights for blacks* to avoid confusion. Historically *civil rights* is a term used mainly to describe the Civil Rights Movement of the 1950s and 1960s, not the 1850s.

Some readers will no doubt be curious about the emphasis put on social class by the primary sources referred to or quoted from in this book, including Elizabeth Jennings, who refers to herself as "respectable" and "genteel." This was typical of the way members of the middle class, both white and black, described themselves in the era.

Other words, archaic in meaning today, are explained in the text or in footnotes when needed.

PART I

A DAY LIKE NO OTHER

The only known photograph of Elizabeth Jennings.

ONE

"Those Monsters in Human Form"

Miss Elizabeth Jennings had a job to do.

She had to get to the First Colored American Congregational Church, where she was the organist. The choir would be waiting for her. They rehearsed each Sunday afternoon, and having the organist accompany them was essential.

But on this particular Sunday she never arrived.

This was surprising. A schoolteacher as well as an accomplished musician, Elizabeth Jennings lived a well-ordered life. In her twenties and unmarried, the youngest of several children, she lived at home with her father, Thomas L. Jennings, and mother, also named Elizabeth, at 167 Church Street in Manhattan. The Jennings family was part of New York City's small black middle class and was active in civic and religious organizations that promoted the education, well-being, and rights of the city's black population.

There was no way of knowing, of course, that this would be a day like no other, that soon she would become embroiled in an incident involving several men she would later call "those monsters in human form." The day's events would change her life—and, as it turned out, the path that history has taken.

THE NATIONAL COLORED CONVENTION IN SESSION AT V

A gathering of black activists in the mid-1800s.

Traveling to church meant a short walk followed by a ride on a streetcar. As she made her way to the streetcar stop, her only concern was being late.

The date was July 16, 1854.

And the place, New York City.

NEW YORK WAS NOT the city it is today, where tall buildings seem to reach into the clouds and subways whisk people from place to place.

There was no Brooklyn Bridge or Statue of Liberty in 1854. They hadn't been built yet. The same was true of the Empire State Building and Rockefeller Center. Times Square, then called Long Acre Square,

was only partially developed.

New York City was made up of Manhattan only. The heavily forested area north that became the Bronx was then a part of Westchester County. Brooklyn was a separate city. Queens was still largely farmland, although factories were starting to be built. On Staten Island a manufacturing boom had not yet begun. Staten Island residents worked mainly on farms or at sea.

The city that Elizabeth Jennings lived in was much smaller, and much dirtier, than it is today. Many roads were unpaved. Some were made of cobblestone. Sidewalks existed in some places but not others.

As she made her way to the streetcar stop at what was then the corner of Pearl and Chatham streets (now the corner of Pearl Street and Park Row), she would have walked around piles of horse manure and maybe even the bloated remains of a dead animal or two—frequently a horse—that had been left to rot. It wasn't uncommon for two to three feet of garbage to be piled up in front of buildings.

To make matters worse, women of the time wore long dresses that came down to the ankle. Elizabeth had to navigate these streets while trying to keep the hem of her dress clean.

A photograph of a crowded and filthy street in Five Points.

This was not harmless dust. This was *foul, disgusting* dirt. Dangerous dirt that was full of germs. That's because there was no indoor plumbing and no city-wide sewer system. Most people lived in four- or five-story apartment buildings and shared crude outhouses with as many as a hundred other residents. Elizabeth's parents owned their home, which meant the Jennings family probably had a private outhouse (called a privy) in a very small backyard.

When it rained, the roadways turned into mud almost instantly. Carriages and wagons became stuck for hours. Raw sewage floated down the street.

On that particular afternoon, as Elizabeth walked to the streetcar stop, rain was not the concern. In fact, there was a drought. In the countryside crops were failing. In the city the air stank and was filled with grit and dust.

Even at the best of times life in the city was very hard for most people. Disease was a regular concern. Deadly cholera epidemics occurred almost every year, including an 1849 outbreak that killed five thousand New Yorkers. Typhus was epidemic in 1852. Tuberculosis was a constant threat. More than half the babies born in the city died before their first birthdays.

The rowdiest, unhealthiest, and most dangerous part of Manhattan was a neighborhood called Five Points, which had such a bad reputation that it had become well known around the world. During a visit to America the famous English author Charles Dickens compared Five Points with the worst slums of London, which he had written about in novels such as *Oliver Twist*. "[H]ideous tenements which take their name from robbery and murder; all that is loathsome, drooping, and decayed is here," Dickens wrote.

Many New Yorkers, if they could avoid it, never went to Five Points. Elizabeth Jennings, whose family lived in a residential neighborhood near the corner of Church and Chamber streets, had to walk through or by this notorious section of Manhattan to catch a streetcar on the Third Avenue Railroad line, which would take her to church.

A famous depiction of Five Points, from the archives of the New-York Historical Society.

As Elizabeth walked to the streetcar stop, she met up with Sarah E. Adams, about whom little is known other than that she was a friend of Elizabeth's. The two women continued on their way together.

As it turned out, Sarah's presence would be very important: She would become the main witness to the events that were about to unfold.

The First New Yorkers

Manhattan was a pristine landscape of meadows, gentle slopes, streams, and marshland for many thousands of years.

The people living there, often called the original New Yorkers, were the Lenni-Lenape, who called it Mannahatta, or "island of the hills."

And then, in 1614, the Dutch came, followed by the English in 1664. The island of the hills would never be the same.

The colonists, enthralled by one of the largest natural harbors in the world, quickly built settlements, starting in lower Manhattan. As time went on, they moved northward and even outward, filling the bogs and marshes of the island with rocks and debris. This was the beginning of New York City, a community called New Amsterdam by the Dutch and then New-York by the English.

The Lenni-Lenape people, whose territory stretched from Manhattan Island south to the Delaware Bay, including all of New Jersey and eastern Pennsylvania, were under siege. Those living on Manhattan were pushed farther north on the island and eventually across the Hudson River (as it was later called) to New Jersey. Some were enslaved. Many died from diseases brought by the Europeans or were killed outright.

The Lenni-Lenape people have not disappeared completely, however. The most substantial populations live on reservations at Bartlesville and Anadarko, Oklahoma, and at Six Nations, Moraviantown, and Muncy Town in Ontario, Canada. Others live in Kansas, Colorado, Ohio, and Wisconsin. The largest and most vibrant community still living in part of the original Lenni-Lenape territory is the Nanticoke Lenni-Lenape Tribal Nation of Bridgeton, New Jersey.

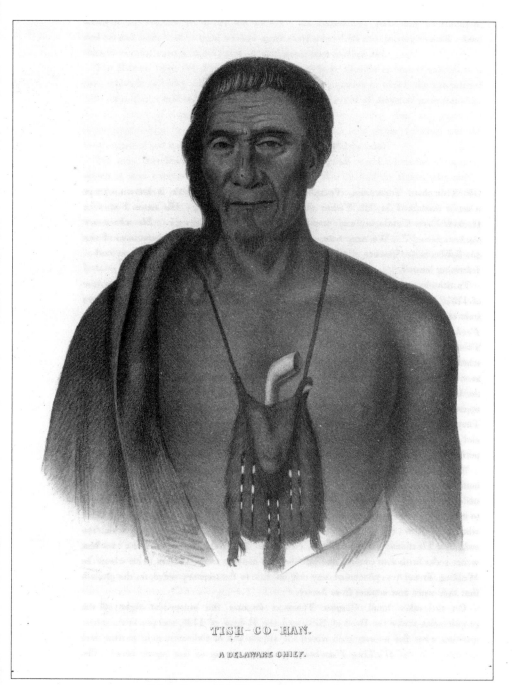

TISH-CO-HAN.

A DELAWARE CHIEF.

Tish-Co-Han, a chief of the Lenni-Lenape people.

TWO

Stray Dogs and Pickpockets

Elizabeth Jennings and Sarah Adams would probably have been looking forward to their streetcar ride. Although sometimes overcrowded, a streetcar was usually the most pleasant way to travel.

Pulled by a team of horses, the streetcars (also called horsecars or trolleys) moved along at eight miles per hour. The ride was smooth and steady because the streetcars were transported on iron or steel rails that had been set into the ground. Each car was operated by at least two men, a driver in charge of the horses and a conductor. Some of the streetcars featured outside seats or places to stand, like a little platform or running board.

Top left: A horse-drawn streetcar in New York.
Bottom left: The conductor and driver (in charge of the horses)

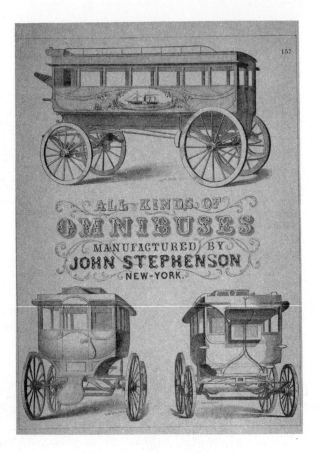

An advertisement for omnibuses, from the collection of the New-York Historical Society.

Compared with an omnibus, which was simply a cart or wagon pulled by a horse, the streetcar was a big improvement. In an omnibus, or even a fancy private carriage, passengers were bounced and jolted with every bump.

Another advantage of the streetcar was that it pulled up to a platform. This made boarding faster and easier for passengers. In the twenty years since the first streetcar line was launched, the service had become very popular. As many as fourteen streetcar (or railroad) companies were said to be operating in Manhattan by 1860.

The streetcar that Elizabeth and Sarah would take was the Third Avenue line.

A horse-drawn streetcar in New York. Photo courtesy of the New-York Historical Society.

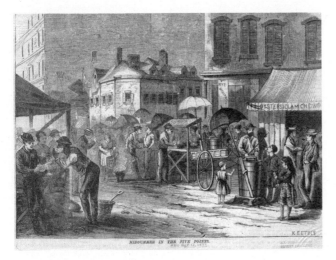

MIDSUMMER IN THE FIVE POINTS.

Top: The corner of Pearl and Chatham streets (now the corner of Pearl Street and Park Row) in 1861. This is where Elizabeth Jennings and Sarah E. Adams boarded the horse-drawn streetcar. Left: Five Points on a midsummer's day. The signs say "Hot Corn," "Rye Bourbon," and "Oysters & Clam Chowder."

This 1859 sketch was called "Pork Lively" and was ironically described by the artist as a "sketch from nature at the corner of Broadway and Fourth Street."

While waiting and watching for a streetcar to pull up, Elizabeth and Sarah would have been surrounded by turmoil. At the intersection of Pearl and Chatham streets, anything could happen. Stray dogs scavenged for food. Wild hogs, a regular nuisance, rooted in the street.

Although it was a Sunday, and businesses in Five Points such as printshops and manufacturers of shoes and tobacco products would be closed, the area would have been bustling with people. Residents trying to escape their hot apartments, visitors from other parts of the city who came out of curiosity, and dockworkers looking for entertainment on their day off created a lively atmosphere.

Peddlers sold all kinds of food and goods. Women typically sold fruit, cakes, and candy similar to jelly beans and chewing gum. Black peddlers specialized in selling buttermilk and straw for bedding. And black women sold a favorite Manhattan treat, hot corn, or freshly cooked ears of sweet corn. These women walked back and forth at intersections, singing:

> "Hot corn all hot, here's your lily white hot corn
> Hot corn all hot, just come out of the boiling pot."

A large number of peddlers and passersby were new immigrants, mostly from Ireland and Germany. Many languages were spoken in the Five Points neighborhood.

To these newly arrived immigrants and even to longtime New Yorkers, it would have been obvious that Elizabeth and Sarah were not poor. Their stylish, clean, and neatly pressed dresses indicated that they were members of the small middle-class black community in New York.

New York was a place of opportunity where, it was said, any young person could rise from a humble background to lead a successful life, with hard work and determination the only requirements. This rags-to-riches dream was later reinforced by the wildly popular writings of Horatio Alger, Jr., a Massachusetts-born author. In his novels, Alger's heroes were street urchins who overcame poverty through courage and good morals.

Left unsaid, however, was the fact that this type of story described a path open to *whites* and to *boys*. Such opportunity was simply not available to girls. For blacks, both boys and girls, the road to success was blocked by the color of their skin. Only a very few managed to break through the barriers, and when they did, they still were not considered equal to whites.

This was the reality Elizabeth and Sarah faced each day of their lives.

Five Points in 1859, from an illustration in the collection of the New-York Historical Society.

Slavery in the North

The institution of slavery was not confined to the southern part of the United States. New York and other northern states were at one time slave states, too.

From 1711 to 1762, a period of fifty-one years, New York City even had its own municipal slave market. Located where Wall Street met the East River, it was where persons of African ancestry, along with some Native Americans, were bought and sold or hired out as day laborers by their owners in a setting no less horrific than the slave markets in such southern cities as Charleston, South Carolina, and Savannah, Georgia.

A drawing of the New York Slave Market at Wall Street.

Enslaved persons were among the workers who built the wall for which Wall Street is named. The construction of the original portion of the city's most famous street, Broadway, included the labor of slaves.

Manhattan is a place of constant change. History is actually paved over. As a result, sometimes New Yorkers are surprised by stark reminders of the past.

One such moment occurred in 1991, when an old burial ground was discovered during the construction of a new federal building at 290 Broadway in lower Manhattan. The burial ground had been the final resting place for thousands of Africans, both free and enslaved, who had died between the 1690s and 1794. In 1993 the site, known as the African Burial Ground, was designated a National Historic Landmark. On February 27, 2006, President George W. Bush named the African Burial Ground a National Monument.

The story of slavery in the United States is complex and far-reaching. In the North slavery ended much sooner than in the South, and it was abolished by the will, or choice, of the people. State by state in the North, citizens supported the passage of laws to stop it.

Vermont, in 1777, was the first state to end slavery. In New York State, people voted to abolish slavery in 1799, but it wasn't stopped overnight. It was phased out gradually until 1827, a period of almost thirty years.

Meanwhile, slavery continued in the South and was the major cause of the Civil War, which lasted from 1861 to 1865. All slaves in southern states in rebellion against the Union were declared free in 1863, when President Abraham Lincoln signed the Emancipation Proclamation. Cementing that decision was the victory of the North (the Union) in the war.

Although slavery was abolished in the North prior to the South, northern states were still deeply entwined with, and profiting in many ways, from southern slavery. Cotton farmed by slaves on southern plantations, to name just one example, was purchased by northern millowners to produce clothing and other products.

In both the North and the South a number of black people were living in freedom during the time of slavery. Some enslaved persons freed themselves by escaping their owners. Others were set free for a number of reasons, often at the time of the slave owner's death.

For those who were free, regardless of the reason, life was still very difficult. Visitors to America reported being surprised that even where slavery had been abolished in the North, blacks were segregated, or separated, from whites. The famous French diplomat and historian Alexis de Tocqueville, in his classic 1835 book *Democracy in America*, maintained that discrimination against blacks struck him as worse in the North than in the South.

"The prejudice of race appears to be stronger in the states that have abolished slavery than in those where it still exists," Tocqueville wrote.

Timeline: The End of Slavery in Northern States

Slavery, once abolished, did not always end abruptly. Instead, in five northern states the institution was phased out over a period of years, even decades. The justification for gradual emancipation, as it was called, was that it would give society, especially owners of enslaved persons, a chance to adapt to the change. Here is a general timeframe for the end of slavery in the North.

Vermont is the first state to end slavery: 1777.

Pennsylvania officially (by law) ends slavery in 1780. However, those born before 1780 were slaves for life; if born after 1780, they were freed at age twenty-eight.

Massachusetts ends slavery: 1783.

New Hampshire ends slavery: 1783.

Rhode Island officially ends slavery in 1784. However, those born before 1784 were slaves for life; if born after 1784, they were indentured to their masters until age twenty-one.

Connecticut officially ends slavery in 1784. However, those born before 1784 were slaves for life; if born after 1784, they were indentured to their masters until age twenty-five.

New York begins to officially end slavery in 1799. However, those born before 1799 were slaves for life; if born after 1799, they were indentured to their masters until age twenty-five if female and twenty-eight if male. In 1817 a new law was passed saying all enslaved persons would be free in 1827.

New Jersey officially ends slavery in 1804. However, those born before 1804 were redefined as "apprenticed for life" (involuntary servitude); if born after 1804, they were indentured for twenty-one years if female and twenty-five years if male.

(Maine was admitted to the Union as a free state in the Missouri Compromise in 1820.)

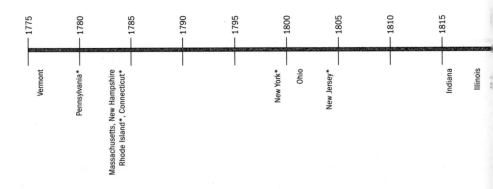

Dates mark the official (by law) end of slavery. States indicated by an asterisk were emancipated gradually.

Before they became states, the following were part of the Northwest Territory created by the Northwest Ordinance (federal law) of 1787, which declared the lands free. However, slavery had been occurring in these areas prior to statehood. As each one applied for statehood, it had, as part of its state constitution, to declare the abolition of slavery. Therefore, each of these states entered the Union as a free state:

Ohio: 1803

Indiana: 1816

Illinois: 1818

Michigan: 1837

Iowa: 1846

Wisconsin: 1848

Minnesota: 1858

States that were not part of the Northwest Territory but also entered the Union as free states were the following:

California: 1850

Oregon: 1859

Kansas, after struggles over slavery that led it to become known as Bleeding Kansas: 1861

Nevada: 1864

West Virginia was admitted as a slave state in 1863 but ended slavery ten months prior to the passage of the Thirteenth Amendment, which abolished slavery and made all states free on December 6, 1865.

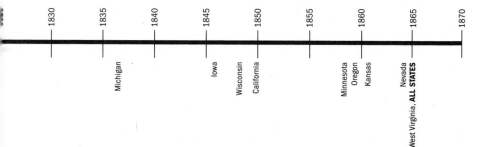

THREE

—

A City Divided by Race

How were black New Yorkers discriminated against?

In every way imaginable New York was a city where segregation (the separation of people by race) and disenfranchisement (a denial of a person's rights) were a way of life. Black New Yorkers were second-class citizens.

An important example of disenfranchisement (and the way the term is usually used) involved the right to vote. Every state that joined the Union after 1819 denied blacks the right to vote. That didn't change until 1870, when the Fifteenth Amendment to the U.S. Constitution was passed. Prior to that, only in Maine, Vermont, New Hampshire, Rhode Island, and Massachusetts did blacks have the right to vote without restriction.

Black chimney sweeps in New York. Because of
discrimination in hiring, black men and women were
typically stuck with the most difficult and dirty jobs.

In New York before 1821, both black and white men could vote if they owned $100 worth of property. After 1821, all white men—not just those who owned property—could vote, but black men had to own $250 worth of property. Since only a handful of black men in the entire state met that requirement, the vast majority were blocked from casting a ballot.

(Meanwhile, regardless of their race, women were not allowed to vote at all. The fight for women's right to vote was a long and difficult struggle that didn't succeed until 1920, when the Nineteenth Amendment to the U.S. Constitution was passed. Even then, many black women were prevented from voting.)

Segregation meanwhile can occur in several ways. When dictated and enforced under the law, it is legal segregation, also called de jure or "under the law." However, segregation can also be de facto ("in fact"), or by custom.

An example of de facto segregation occurred in public education in New York. An 1841 state law declared that all children age five to sixteen could attend a district school if they lived in that district. Yet black children did not often attend school alongside white children because the officials in charge were allowed to open separate schools for black children, and they often did. When it came time to distribute funds, schools for black children received far less money. They were "dark, damp, small, and cheerless" places, according to one newspaper account.

Another example of de facto segregation was in hiring practices. Many jobs, for example, were not open to blacks. Racist white employers simply would not consider hiring them, and there were no laws in place to make them do so.

Blacks who wanted to be professionals became ministers (a position then open only to men) or teachers. Only a small number of people were able to acquire the education needed to qualify for a teaching position. Elizabeth Jennings, according to one record, was one of just thirteen black teachers in New York City in 1855, and that number included men.

Those who dreamed of becoming bankers, doctors, or lawyers found it all but impossible. One educated young black man expressed his sadness and frustration. "What are my prospects?" he wrote in a letter that has often been cited by historians. "No one will have me in his office; white boys won't work with me. Shall I be a merchant? No one will have me; white clerks won't associate with me."

Even the poorest white immigrants could rise from poverty faster than black New Yorkers. Not that it was easy, but it could be done, even with the burden of having to learn English. For blacks, education was not the key to success that it was for whites.

As a result, male black New Yorkers had no choice but to take the hardest and lowest-paying jobs, such as chimney sweeps, laborers, servants, mariners (working on the docks or on ships), barbers, coachmen, and cooks.

Black women had even fewer options. Other than peddling goods on the street, the most common ways to make a living were cooking, cleaning, and doing washing. Sometimes these jobs meant living away from their families. Those who were hired as live-in servants, for example, moved to their employers' homes. The only time they spent with their own families was one day a week, on Sunday.

Even in churches there was segregation, with black worshippers often forced to sit in a balcony or on a back pew. Black New Yorkers responded by starting their own churches, including the First Colored American Congregational Church, on Sixth Street near the Bowery, where Elizabeth was headed on July 16, 1854.

Blacks and whites did not mingle openly except in the poorest neighborhoods, such as Five Points. Segregation in housing was common and on the rise. By 1852, 86 percent of black residents lived below Fourteenth Street, almost half of them in a single area that included parts of the Third, Fifth, and Eighth wards. The Jennings family home on Church Street was in the Fifth Ward. Three-quarters of Manhattan streets did not have any black residents at all. Black New

Yorkers reported feeling stared at and uncomfortable in many parts of the city.

Theaters were segregated, with black patrons usually sold seats in a separate section far from the stage. There were stores where black New Yorkers were not welcome, and they were barred as customers from most hotels and restaurants.

And if blacks in New York wanted to take a streetcar, they encountered rules that forced them to ride on the outside of the car or to wait for one displaying a sign that stated COLORED PEOPLE ALLOWED IN THE CAR. The "colored" streetcars were often called Jim Crow cars, an insulting term used by whites to describe black people.

Jim Crow cars often came late, if they came at all. Conductors of cars meant for whites only (which did not carry a sign saying "white" but were simply unlabeled) would sometimes allow a black passenger to board if none of the white passengers objected—and if the conductor felt like it.

Segregated streetcars were a source of great frustration for black New Yorkers. As Manhattan expanded, the streetcar system became more important for getting to work. Each time Elizabeth, or any black person, needed to get somewhere by streetcar, the uncertainty surrounding the journey was stressful. Black New Yorkers could leave home early and still arrive late.

On that summer day Elizabeth, standing beside Sarah, was feeling that pressure. According to her own written account, all she wanted was to get to choir rehearsal on time. A streetcar finally came into view, and she held up her hand to signal the driver to stop. Although it was an unmarked streetcar meant for whites, she hoped the conductor would be understanding and let them ride.

With Sarah right behind her, she stepped up onto the platform, ready to make her case.

What Was Jim Crow?

Jim Crow was the name of a character in a minstrel show, a type of performance in which a singer, accompanied by music, tells a story. While minstrel shows date back hundreds of years, the Jim Crow character, which depicted an insulting portrait of a black man, became popular in the United States starting in the late 1820s.

Jim Crow and the other minstrel characters were played by whites with their hands and faces blackened with soot. The popularity of minstrel shows in New York helped launch the Jim Crow character nationally.

Over time the term *Jim Crow* began to be used to refer to segregation. Streetcars in New York City meant for blacks were often called Jim Crow cars, according to the book *Gotham*, Edwin G. Burrows's and Mike Wallace's Pulitzer Prize–winning book on New York history. The term is most closely associated with racist laws that were passed to restrict blacks in the post–Civil War South. So-called Jim Crow laws created separate (and inferior) facilities in every part of society, including schools, hospitals, and transportation. Public rest rooms and drinking fountains in the South were labeled "Whites Only" and "Colored."

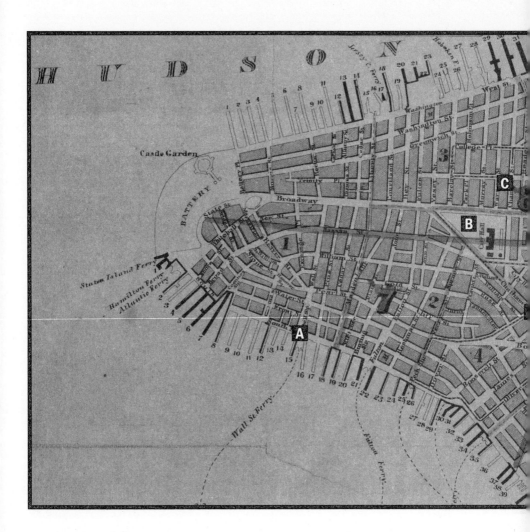

Manhattan Map 1856

A street map of lower Manhattan from 1856 showing:

A. New York's Slave Market at Wall Street, which was in operation from 1711 to 1762.

B. City Hall.

C. The Jennings family home at 167 Church Street.

D. The center of Five Points.

E. The intersection of Pearl and Chatham streets, where Elizabeth and her friend Sarah boarded the streetcar. Chatham was later renamed Park Row.

F. The corner of Walker Street and the Bowery, known today as Bowery and Canal, where Elizabeth was ejected a second time.

G. First Colored American Congregational Church, on Sixth Street near Bowery, where Elizabeth had been headed on July 16, 1854.

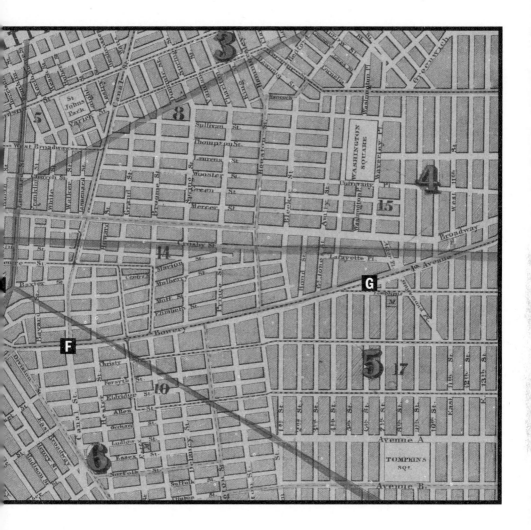

Elizabeth Jennings as a young woman.

FOUR

"I Screamed Murder with All My Voice"

THE CONDUCTOR SAID NO.

Elizabeth tried to explain her situation. In her mind it was a perfectly reasonable request.

"I told him that I could not wait, as I was in a hurry to go to church and the other car was about a block off," she wrote later. "He then told me that the other car had my people in it, that it was appropriated* for that purpose. I then told him I had no people; it was no particular occasion, I wished to go to church, as I had been going for the last six months, and I did not wish to be detained."

The conductor, however, would not change his mind. "He insisted upon my getting off the car," Elizabeth wrote. "I told him I would wait on the car until the other car came up. He again insisted on my waiting in the street, but I did not get off.

"By this time the other car came up, and I asked the driver if there was any room in his car," she continued. "He told me very distinctly, No, that there was more room in my car than there was in his, yet this did not satisfy the conductor. He still kept driving me out or off of the car and said he had as much time as I had and could wait just as long."

---

* *"set aside"*   35

Elizabeth did not give up. "I replied, 'Very well, we'll see.' He waited some few minutes, when the driver* becoming impatient, he said to me, 'Well, you may go in, but remember, if the passengers raise any objections you shall go out, whether or not, I'll put you out.' I answered again and told him I was a respectable person, born and raised in New-York, did not know where he was born, that I had never been insulted before while going to church, and that he was a good for nothing impudent fellow for insulting decent persons while on their way to church."

The conductor told her that he was from Ireland, although that made no difference to Elizabeth. "I made answer it made no difference where a man was born, that he was none the worse or better for that, provided he behaved himself and did not insult genteel persons," she wrote.

Her words enraged the conductor.

"He then said I should come out** [or] he would put me out***. I told him not to lay his hands on me," she wrote. "He took hold of me and I took hold of the window sash and held on. He pulled me until he broke my grasp and I took hold of his coat and held onto that. He also broke my grasp**** but previously he had dragged my companion***** out, she all the while screaming for him to let go. He then ordered the driver to fasten his horses, which he did, and come and help him put me out of the car. They then both seized hold of me by the arms and pulled and dragged me flat down on the bottom of the platform, so that my feet hung one way and my head the other, nearly on the ground.

"I screamed murder with all my voice, and my companion screamed out 'You'll kill her, don't kill her.' The driver then let go of me and went to his horses."

But this would not be the end of the violent encounter. What happened next surprised Sarah, the conductor, and probably everyone on the streetcar.

* *of the horses*
** *of the car*
*** *onto the street*
**** *of the coat*
***** *Sarah*

FIVE

"You Will Sweat for This!"

ELIZABETH JENNINGS HAD A CHOICE TO MAKE. Most people probably would have backed down. Most people, when physically assaulted by someone much bigger and stronger, would retreat.

But Elizabeth Jennings was not "most people."

To everyone's amazement, she got up and returned to the streetcar. Her friend, Sarah, stayed behind, watching from the sidewalk.

Once on the streetcar Elizabeth found a seat.

And she sat down.

The conductor reacted with fury. As Elizabeth recalled, "He said, 'You will sweat for this!' Then he told the driver to drive as fast as he could and not take another passenger in the car, to drive until he saw an officer or a Station House."

At the corner of Walker Street and the Bowery (known today as the Bowery and Canal Street) a policeman was spotted, and the streetcar came to a halt. Elizabeth stayed where she was, but she could hear the conversation.

"The conductor told* that his orders from the agent** were to admit colored persons if the passengers did not object, but if they did, not to let them ride," she wrote.

* _the policeman_
** _the conductor's employer,_
the railroad company

37

"The officer, without listening to anything I had to say, thrust me out, and then pushed me, and tauntingly told me to get redress* if I could," she continued. "The conductor gave me [his] name and [the] number of his car; he wrote his name as Moss and the streetcar, No. 7, but I looked and saw No. 6 on the back of the car. After dragging me off the car he drove me away like a dog, saying not to be talking there and raising a mob or fight."

The streetcar continued on its way, leaving Elizabeth dazed, bruised, and battered.

She got to her feet and brushed herself off. Because Sarah had not gotten back on the streetcar a second time, Elizabeth was alone. After catching her breath, she began walking slowly down Walker Street toward home, which was about three-quarters of a mile away.

"A German gentleman followed," Elizabeth wrote. "He told me he saw the whole transaction in the street as he was passing" and offered to be a witness. On a piece of paper the man, who was a bookseller on Pearl Street, wrote down his name and address so that she could contact him later.

When she arrived at home, Elizabeth's parents were shocked at the sight of her. They sent for a doctor immediately. The doctor, whose name we do not know, arrived quickly. He examined her and concluded that she had suffered many bruises, cuts, and scratches and probably broken bones from being twice removed by force from the streetcar, first, when she was dragged off the car by the conductor and driver and a second time, when she was pushed by the policeman. He told her that she must have complete bed rest. Elizabeth's father instructed her to write down, in her own words, an account of what had happened, with as much detail as possible. Propped up in bed, Elizabeth wrote a letter describing her version of events.

Then her father left the house in a hurry. With Elizabeth's written statement in his hand, he disappeared into the city.

SIX

An Admired Family

Wɪᴛʜɪɴ ʜᴏᴜʀs ᴏғ ᴛʜᴇ ᴀssᴀᴜʟᴛ Elizabeth's father had traveled throughout lower Manhattan and shown her letter to the black leaders of New York.

Thomas Jennings had protested racial injustice many times in his life. As a young man he had marched with others through the streets of lower Manhattan, and he had joined and supported numerous organizations that advocated for the members of his race.

But this time the incident was deeply personal. His own daughter had been not only insulted but attacked and injured. He would help her in any way he could.

As an activist himself he knew where to turn for help. He reached out to his friends, an influential group that included the most famous black leader in America at the time, Frederick Douglass.

The organizations to which Thomas Jennings belonged make an impressive list. He had been present at the first, second, and third National Conventions of Free People of Color (sometimes also called the National Conventions of Colored Men), held in Philadelphia in 1830, 1831, and 1832. He was a founder of the Wilberforce Philanthropic Society, a black self-help organization named after the British abolitionist (antislavery advocate) William Wilberforce.

He was a founder, also, of the Abyssinian Baptist Church and an organization called the Phoenix Society, launched in 1833 "to promote the improvement of the colored people in morals, literature, and the mechanic arts."

By profession Thomas Jennings was a tailor and self-made businessman. He got his break as a young man when he was apprenticed to a successful tailor, whose name has been lost to time. Eventually Thomas owned his own shop, located at Nassau and Chatham streets.

Thomas Jennings was also an inventor. In 1821 or so, he was awarded a patent from the U.S. government for developing a new method to dry-clean clothing. He was perhaps the first black person to receive a patent.

Although he was treated as a second-class citizen because of the color of his skin, Thomas Jennings was a patriotic man who loved his country, according to Frederick Douglass, who wrote a tribute to Jennings after his death. During the War of 1812 Jennings had volunteered to dig trenches on Long Island that would help the American forces fighting the British, and his most-prized possession was the patent he was awarded by the U.S. government and signed by John Quincy Adams, the secretary of state and future president.

As a young man Thomas Jennings married a woman named Elizabeth Cartwright, whose father, Jacob, had been a black soldier in the Revolutionary War.

The couple had at least five children—William, Thomas Jr., Matilda, Lucy, and Elizabeth (named after her mother).

Frederick Douglass in a photograph taken in 1880. He wrote admiringly of Elizabeth Jennings, saying that her conduct was "courageous" and "beyond all praise."

THE COLORED AMERICAN.

VOL. I.   "RIGHTEOUSNESS EXALTETH A NATION."   NO. 38.

SAMUEL E. CORNISH, Editor.   New-York, Saturday, September 23, 1837.   PHILIP A. BELL, Proprietor.

The following is one of the Addresses on the occasion.

ON THE IMPROVEMENT OF THE MIND.

Friends, in appearing before you this evening, I find words inadequate to express my feelings, for the honor conferred on me of addressing you, in the celebration of this anniversary. I am conscious of my incapacity to do justice to the task allotted me. But as our object is improvement, and feeling that yours is the same, we have but to solicit your kind indulgence.

It is now a momentous time, a time that calls us to exert all our powers, and among the many of them, the mind is the greatest, and great care should be taken to improve it with diligence. We should cultivate those powers and dispositions of the mind, which may prove advantageous to us. It is impossible to attain to that sphere for which we were created, without persevering. It is certain we were formed for society, and it is our duty and interest to cultivate social qualities and dispositions—to endeavor to make ourselves useful and pleasing to others—to promote and encourage their happiness—to cherish the friendly affections, that we may find in them the source of the greatest blessings this world can afford.

But, alas! society too often exhibits a far different scene, and this is in consequence of neglect of cultivation, which certainly is much more fatal than we can imagine. Neglect will plunge us into deeper degradation, and keep us grovelling in the dust, while our enemies will rejoice and say, we do not believe they (colored people) have any minds; if they have, they are unsusceptible of improvement. My sisters, allow me to ask the question, shall we bring this reproach on ourselves? Doubtless you answer NO, we will strive to avoid it. But hark! methinks I hear the well known voice of Abigail A. Matthews, saying you can avoid it. Why sleep thus? Awake and slumber no more—arise, put on your armor, ye daughters of America, and stand forth in the field of improvement. You can all do some good, and if you do but little it will increase in time. The mind is powerful, and by its efforts your influence may be as near perfection, as that of those which have extended over kingdoms, and is applauded by thousands.

Let us accord with that voice which we hear urging us, and resolve to adorn our minds with a more abundant supply of those gems for which we have united ourselves—nor let us ever think any occasion too trifling for our best endeavors. It is by constant aiming at perfection in every thing, that we may at length attain to it.

At right, the original 1837 newspaper clipping of the speech "On the Improvement of the Mind," recited by ten-year-old Elizabeth Jennings.

Also living in the family home were boarders who rented rooms, a common practice at the time. Among those who stayed with the family were black teachers, seamstresses, and at least one doctor.

Elizabeth and her siblings attended one of the African Free Schools founded by the New York Manumission Society, an antislavery group. The Jennings children were fortunate compared with most American children, black and white. At that time many children did not go to school.

The Jennings children also were expected to participate in civic groups that aimed to improve conditions for blacks. In the fall of 1837, at the age of ten, Elizabeth, for example, recited an essay to an audience of adults at a meeting of the Ladies' Literary Society of the City of New York. This was an organization of black women who promoted literacy and self-improvement as the way to advancement.

Speaking to a roomful of adults may sound like a formidable task for many ten-year-olds, but recitation (repeating something aloud from memory) was a learning technique then commonly used by educators. Recitations by children were even a form of popular entertainment, which the author Charles Dickens poked fun of with his character the Infant Phenomenon in *The Life and Adventures of Nicholas Nickleby*.

The essay recited by Elizabeth, titled "On the Improvement of the Mind," contends that the path to a successful life is through education, learning, and "the constant aiming of perfection."

While almost certainly written by an adult, possibly her mother, who may have belonged to the organization, Elizabeth proudly delivered the address, which was published afterward in *The Colored American* newspaper. The audience was inspired. These were bold words at a time when the very idea would have been radical for a black child, especially one who was female. Recited by a young black girl, the words had an impact on listeners.

Elizabeth Jennings, at the age of ten, was already learning to try hard, to aim high, and, with courage and confidence, to fight the racial prejudice that so unfairly held black people back.

Frederick Douglass and the Black Press

Frederick Douglass was an extraordinary American and the most famous black person of his time. Born into slavery in Maryland in 1817, he escaped to Massachusetts as a young man. While in his early twenties he was asked to give an impromptu speech at a meeting of the Massachusetts Anti-Slavery Society. He made such a strong impression that he was recruited immediately to deliver lectures arguing against slavery.

Douglass was not only a brilliant public speaker but an outstanding writer and journalist. His autobiography, *Narrative of the Life of Frederick Douglass*, published in 1845, was read widely. Two years later he started his own abolitionist newspaper, *The North Star*, in Rochester, New York. He renamed the publication *Frederick Douglass' Paper*, which he published from 1851 to 1860. In January 1859 he started *Douglass' Monthly*.

He was among several black men who launched groundbreaking newspapers. John B. Russwurm, Rev. Samuel Cornish, William Hamilton, and Rev. Peter Williams, Jr., started *Freedom's Journal*, the first black newspaper in the U.S. Published in New York from 1827 to 1829, the paper was edited by Russwurm and Cornish.

From 1837 to 1841 a black newspaper titled *The Colored American* (called, for a short time, *The Weekly Advocate*) was published by Cornish. Others published in New York State in the 1840s or 1850s included *The Elevator*, *National Watchman*, *People's Press*, *Ram's Horn*, *The Colored Man's Journal*, and *The Anglo-African*.

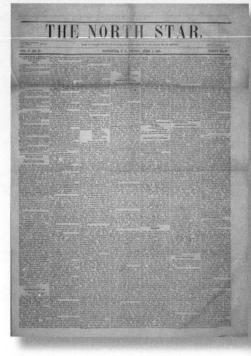

The front page of an issue of Frederick Douglass's abolitionist newspaper, *The North Star*.

Frederick Douglass' Paper.

VOL. VII.—NO. 40.   ROCHESTER, N. Y. FRIDAY, SEPTEMBER 22, 1854.   WHOLE NO. 392.

But Douglass's publications were the most well known of them all. Through his writings, along with his lectures, he made an enormous contribution to the fight against slavery. His goal was not only freedom for the enslaved but social and economic equality for all blacks. His chronicles included writings about people who were taking action in an admirable way. Among them was the young New York City schoolteacher named Elizabeth Jennings, whose conduct he called "courageous" and "beyond all praise."

For Frederick Douglass' Paper.

The following preamble and resolution, was presented by J. R. STARKEY, before the Young Men's Association of San Francisco, Cal., August 14th, 1854, and unanimously passed :—

Whereas, We have learned by the New York *Tribune* of July 19th, that two colored ladies, ELIZABETH JENNINGS and SARAH E. ADAMS, were violently ejected from a public conveyance into the street, by a ruffianly Irish driver in the city of New York, solely on account of their color, while on their way to *Church,* upon the Sabbath ; and,

Whereas, We cannot believe that such outrages upon the rights, and persons of intelligent and upright citizens, will be sanctioned by the public, when they shall be made aware of their perpetration, but that they will denounce, and command that such outrages shall no longer be permitted ; therefore,

Resolved, That we have read with deep interest the proceedings of the meeting of colored citizens of New York, in relation to the brutal treatment Misses JENNINGS and ADAMS were subjected to, and heartily approve the course pursued by our brethren at that meeting, and sympathize with the ladies, who were the subjects of the treatment complained of ; and we say to our friends, even from the distant shores of the Pacific, that we, with them, do, and will ever protest against this, and like injustice on all proper occasions, and resist it by all proper means, by appealing to justice and importuning public sentiment, until we secure our rights.

On motion of Mr. TAYLOR, the Secretary was directed to forward on a copy of the resolution to F. DOUGLASS' PAPER, with a request to publish the same.

J. FRANCIS, *Sec'y pro tem.*

SAN FRANCISCO, August 14th, 1854.

A letter from a San Francisco group in support of Elizabeth Jennings, published in *Frederick Douglass' Paper.*

Who Should Go to School?

There was a time when children in the United States did not have to go to school. Public education for all was a social movement that gathered momentum in the second half of the 1800s. Before that time going to school was a privilege for children whose parents could pay for it. Going to school, for the lucky few whose parents could afford it, meant attending a private academy, such as the African Free School, where Elizabeth Jennings and her siblings were enrolled.

The children of most free blacks as well as poor and working-class whites had to work to support their families. In rural communities these children labored on the family farm, from harvesting crops and milking cows to hauling water, cooking, washing clothes, and other chores to keep the household running. In cities children of peddlers carried goods for sale on their backs. Children also worked in factories to help their parents make ends meet. Some of these jobs were very dangerous, and laws that would make it illegal to hire children did not yet exist.

Some families who could afford to send their children to school chose to send their sons but not their daughters. When girls were allowed to attend school, it was often believed that their education, with an emphasis on a liberal arts curriculum, should prepare them to be better mothers and wives, and most important, to nurture better-educated sons.

New York African Free School, right, in a drawing by a student named John Burns. Courtesy of New-York Historical Society.

Some educators strongly believed that girls had no place in the classroom at all. Others restricted them for reasons that seem frivolous today. Girls were seen as delicate and in need of protection. Classrooms for young women were sometimes even held on the lower floors of buildings because climbing flights of stairs was thought to be a danger to a girl's health.

A classroom in a school for black children in New York in 1861. Courtesy of the New-York Historical Society.

NEW-YORK TRIBUNE.

New-York Daily Tribune.

V. XIV....N. 4.134.   NEW-YORK, WEDNESDAY, JULY 19, 1854.   PRICE TWO CENTS.

OUTRAGE UPON COLORED PERSONS.

At a public meeting held in pursuance of due notice given of the colored citizens of the City and County of New-York, in the First Colored American Congregational Church, in Sixth-st., near the Bowery, for the purpose of making an expression of public sentiment condemnatory of the outrage committed upon the person of Miss Elizabeth Jennings, a highly respectable female, (who is employed as a teacher in the male department of one of the public schools in this City; also organist in the above-named church, in Sixth-st.,) while on her way to church on Sabbath afternoon, July 16, when she was most brutally outraged and insulted by a conductor of one of the Third-av. City cars.

The meeting was called to order, whereupon the Rev. Levis Tilmon was appointed Chairman and P. S. Ewell, Secretary.

The Chairman stated the object of the assembly, after which the Rev. James Vickes of New-York addressed the meeting, and made a very elaborate speech appropriate to the occasion.

The Secretary then read a statement from Miss E. Jennings, which was presented in writing, she being unable to attend the meeting, owing to the injuries received at the hands of the railroad conductor and his abetors. The statement is as follows:

Sarah E. Adams and myself walked down to the corner of Pearl and Chatham sts. to take the Third-av. cars; I held up my hand to the driver and he stopped the cars; we got on the platform, when the conductor told us to wait for the next car; I told him I could not wait, as I was in a hurry to go to church, (the other car was about a block off;) he then told me that the other car had my people in it, that it was appropriated for that purpose; I then told him I had no people; it was no particular occasion; I wished to go to church, as I had been going for the last six months, and I did not wish to be detained; he insisted upon upon my getting off the car; I told him I would wait on the car until the other car came up; he again insisted on my waiting in the street, but I did not get off the car; by this time the other car came up, and I asked the driver if there was any room in his car; he told me very distinctly, "No, that there was more room in my car than "there was in his;" yet this did not satisfy the conductor; he still kept driving me out or off of the car; said he had as much time as I had and could wait just as long; I replied, "Very well, we'll see;" he waited some few minutes, when the drivers becoming impatient, he said to me, "Well, you may go in, but remember, if the passen- "gers raise any objections you shall go out, whether

"or no, or I'll put you out;" I answered again and told him I was a respectable person, born and raised in New-York, did not know where he was born, that I had never been insulted before while going to church, and that he was a good for nothing impudent fellow for insulting decent persons while on their way to church; he then said I should come out and he would put me out; I told him not to lay his hands on me; he took hold of me and I took hold of the window sash and held on; he pulled me until he broke my grasp and I took hold of his coat and held on to that, he also broke my grasp from that, (but previously he had dragged my companion out, she all the while screaming for him to let go;) he then ordered the driver to fasten his horses, which he did, and come and help him put me out of the car; they then both seized hold of me by the arms and pulled and dragged me flat down on the bottom of the platform, so that my feet hung one way and my head the other, nearly on the ground. I screamed murder with all my voice, and my companion screamed out "you'll kill her; don't kill her;" the driver then let go of me and went to his horses; I went again in the car, and the conductor said you shall sweat for this; then told the driver to drive as fast as he could and not take another passenger in the car; to drive until he saw an officer or a Station House; they got an officer on the corner of Walker and Bowery, whom the conductor told that his orders from the agent were to admit colored persons if the passengers did not object, but if they did, not to let them ride; when the officer took me there were some eight or ten persons in the car; when the officer, without listening to anything I had to say, thrust me out, and then pushed me, and tauntingly told me to get redress if I could; this the conductor also told me, and gave me some name and number of his car; he wrote his name Moss and the car No. 7, but I looked and saw No. 6 on the back of the car; after dragging me off the car he drove me away like a dog, saying, not to be talking there and raising a mob or fight; I came home down Walker-st., and a German gentleman followed, who told me he saw the whole transaction in the street as he was passing; his address is Latour, No. 148 Pearl-st., bookseller; when I told the conductor I did not know where he was born, he answered, "I was born in Ireland;" I made answer it made no difference where a man was born, that he was none the worse or better for that, provided he behaved himself and did not insult genteel persons.

I would have come up myself, but am quite sore and stiff from the treatment I received from those monsters in human form yesterday afternoon. This statement I believe to be correct, and it is respectfully submitted.

ELIZABETH JENNINGS.

The original *New-York Daily Tribune* story that includes Elizabeth Jennings's firsthand account of what happened to her on the fateful afternoon of July 16, 1854.

48

SEVEN

A "Shameful" and "Loathsome" Issue

WORD SPREAD QUICKLY about the assault on Elizabeth Jennings, and an emergency meeting was called at the First Colored American Congregational Church.

Under doctor's orders to stay in bed, Elizabeth was unable to attend the meeting, which was held on either July 17 or 18. "I would have come up myself, but am quite sore and stiff from the treatment I received from those monsters in human form yesterday afternoon," she wrote. Her firsthand description of the assault was read aloud.

Thomas Jennings attended the meeting and added a few observations. What an emotional scene it must have been, with Elizabeth's much-admired father standing in the front of the gathered congregation, speaking about his beloved daughter.

The meeting resulted in a decision: The incident was not going to be shunted aside or forgotten. Five people, including Thomas Jennings, were appointed to a committee that would study the facts and pursue justice.

The committee's first step was to let others know about the assault. Elizabeth's firsthand, written account was delivered to the offices of the *New-York Daily Tribune*, which published it under the headline OUTRAGE UPON COLORED PERSONS on July 19, 1854.

THE LIBERATOR.

VOL. I.   WILLIAM LLOYD GARRISON AND ISAAC KNAPP, PUBLISHERS.   NO. 19.

Boston, Massachusetts.]   OUR COUNTRY IS THE WORLD—OUR COUNTRYMEN ARE MANKIND.   [Saturday, May 7, 1831.

COST OF PREJUDICE.

The manner in which our colored citizens are generally treated by the proprietors of stages and steam-boats, whenever they attempt to go from one town or State to another, is vulgar and shameful in the extreme. If they travel as servants or slaves, in company with their masters or mistresses, no offence is given, and none taken; but as intelligent, virtuous, and independent passengers, they are not permitted to enjoy what is granted to the most rude, profligate, and vulgar whites. We have some facts on this subject to communicate to the public, which ought to make every true American blush for his country. It is a humiliating truth, that prejudice against persons of a colored complexion is more exclusive and venomous in New-England, than in any other portion of this republic. We are consoled, however, in believing—nay, in *knowing*, that it is rapidly declining—precisely in proportion to the growth of the anti-slavery cause.

It may be for the pecuniary advantage of the proprietors of taverns, stages, steamboats, &c. to know that the following resolution was unanimously adopted at the recent meeting of the New-England Anti-Slavery Convention, and that it will find a hearty response in the breasts of thousands of our most respectable fellow citizens.

On motion of David L. Child, Esq. of Boston,

Resolved, That it is the duty of all the friends and well wishers of the anti-slavery cause, to inquire out, and encourage with their custom and their influence, those taverns, stages, and steamboats, which receive and accommodate our colored fellow citizens, without making an illiberal and disgraceful distinction either of charges or of treatment on account of color.

The above furnishes one answer to the sneering question which is so often propounded to abolitionists, 'What do you mean to do?' We mean to destroy prejudice, and to give our colored brother all those rights and privileges which belong to him as a man. And to show that we are in earnest in this matter—that we practice as well as preach—that we execute as well as resolve—and to show, moreover, that prejudice is likely to prove a costly antipathy to its possessor—I subjoin the following letter, which was put into the hands of Capt. Davis of the steam-boat Philadelphia, (People's Line,) plying between Philadelphia and Bristol, and which carries its own explanation with it.

PHILADELPHIA, May 5, 1831.

Adding to the frustration of Elizabeth's supporters was the fact that segregation on the modes of transportation in the Northeast, not just New York City, was a long-standing problem. There were many reports of black travelers, both men and women, who were treated badly and unfairly on northern omnibuses, streetcars, railroads, ships, and steamboats.

Northern abolitionists, who were trying to find ways to end slavery in the South, were embarrassed by these incidents. They are "shameful in the extreme," a white attorney named David L. Child, who belonged to an antislavery organization in Boston, Massachusetts, wrote in a newspaper called *The Liberator*.

An article in an 1831 edition of *The Liberator* on the topic of segregation on modes of transportation in the North.

A lengthy commentary in the September 7, 1850, edition of the *New-York Daily Tribune* by an irate editorial writer who had witnessed an incident on a Manhattan horse-drawn streetcar.

A New-York Incident.

Going up-town in a Harlem car, yesterday, we saw a young woman approach the car to take passage, not thinking of any impediment, when she was decidedly, though without extra insult, repelled by the Conductor, who informed her that she could not be permitted to ride in the car. Stepping to the door to learn the reason of this strange proceeding, (as there were but two or three persons in the car) we saw that the woman was copper-colored, (either half or quarter African by descent) and were informed that this was the reason of her repulse.

"But isn't it a very base reason?"

"Can't help it, sir; the passengers make a fuss and say they can't ride with niggers."

—We fear that is true—yet what a shameful, loathsome, debasing truth it is! Here in this metropolis of Christian America, with at least a regiment of priests and other professed teachers of righteousness and humility, in the midst of two hundred and odd steeples and within sight of half a dozen, a cleanly, respectable looking woman is repelled from a public conveyance, in which there is room enough to place her six feet from any body else, because of her dusky complexion!

Who drove that helpless woman back upon the side-walk, in an agony of chagrin and mortification?

Not the conductor—he was but the passive instrument of others—not the Company—they would have been willing enough to pocket her six-pence, if the Public would have permitted it. But a base and wicked Popular Prejudice, the offspring of Slavery, fostered and stimulated for selfish ends by a deluding and counterfeit party Democracy, countenanced and upheld by our empty and cowardly fashionable Christianity, with negro pews in its Churches and negro quarters at its communion-tables—these are the real culprits who subjected that unoffending woman to insult and ignominy in a street of this Christian Republican metropolis.

Must this class of outrages be perpetuated?

We think not. Nay, we trust they are already outgrown. True, the negro-pews are still maintained in most of our Churches, especially the most costly and stylish, and the Negro-phobia is studiously fomented by our swindling Democracy, so that if a dozen black men should venture into a Democratic City Meeting to listen to the eloquence there poured forth in glorification of Human Freedom and Equality, they would be kicked down stairs in short order—yet still, we believe Public Sentiment is fast outgrowing the Paganism of the Church and the aristocracy of Democracy. We believe our Railroads and Stages might now resolve to carry neat, decently dressed black and copper-colored persons the same as white ones, without any material damage to their interests—that they would hardly lose more passengers than they would gain by so doing, and that after a year or so they would lose none at all. Africans are carried now the same as Whites throughout the greater part of New-England, though twenty years ago the mean prejudice of caste and color was as rank and brutal there as it now is here. And if the Railroads and Stages should once get Christianized in this respect, there would be hope that the Churches might in time be shamed into following the example. As to what vaunts itself 'Democracy,' that is more incorrigible, but it too will knuckle to a purified Public Sentiment. Only let it be understood that more votes can be obtained by Negrophilism than by Negro-phobia, and Fred Douglass will be called to address a Ratifying Convention in Tammany Hall, with two or three of Afric's noblest sons for Vice-Presidents.

—But isn't it a good idea, in view of facts every day transpiring around us, to talk of organizing the whole North into a grand Anti-Slavery party? They who don't see that the spirit of Slavery is as rampant and predominant in New-York as in Virginia know far too little to be trusted with the devising of new parties. Let us purify our own borders before arraying ourselves in a grand crusade against the sins of our neighbors.

He was referring to the way blacks were treated by stagecoach companies and on steamboats throughout the North, not just in Boston or New York. His words were published in 1831, twenty-three years before Elizabeth Jennings was assaulted and ejected from the streetcar in New York City.

Frederick Douglass wrote frequently of routine discrimination against black travelers. On steamboats that traversed the Hudson River, for example, he called the way in which colored persons were uniformly treated "brutal." They are, he noted, "compelled sometimes to stroll the decks nearly all night, before they can get a place to lie down, and that place frequently unfit for a dog's accommodation."

In the fall of 1850 the *New-York Daily Tribune* published the story of an incident observed by an editorial or "opinion" writer, probably a white man. His name is not known. As was the custom with editorials, no byline was given.

The editorial writer had witnessed a conductor refusing to allow a black woman to ride on an uptown streetcar. "Stepping to the door to learn the reason . . . as there were but two or three persons in the car, we saw that the woman was copper-colored, either half or quarter African by descent, and were informed that this was the reason [she was removed]," he wrote.

He questioned the conductor, whom he quoted as saying, "Can't help it, sir; the passengers make a fuss. . . ."

In a lengthy commentary the nameless writer voiced his belief that

A letter to the editor in response to the commentary in the *New-York Daily Tribune*, September 16, 1850.

The Exclusion of Colored Persons from Public Conveyances.

To the Editors of The Tribune:

GENTLEMEN: In *The Tribune* of Saturday, 7th inst. you allude to "A New York Incident," which is of too frequent occurrence, but the reason given by yourself and the conductor for ejecting colored people from our City cars and omnibuses is far from being a true one. In nine cases out of ten the passengers have no objection. I can ride without molestation or any remark whatever in the Brooklyn omnibusses or in the ears of any Railroad except the City cars. In the North River, New-Haven, Harlem, (through line,) Long Island, and all the Jersey lines I am a frequent passenger, and I always take first class cars, and I have never yet been refused a passage, but in our City cars and omnibusses I am either rejected or pointed to an outside seat, which I of course refuse, preferring to walk, although were I free to choose I would often ride outside.

There are a few honorable exceptions. I believe colored persons can ride in most of the Dry Dock stages. I have never been refused a seat in Alderman Conoklin's line, and I also ride unmolested in the Fulton Ferry stages.

I repeat, the objection is *not* with the passengers, but with the proprietors; and too often with the drivers alone, without any prohibition from the proprietors.

A popular omnibus proprietor told me he had never given orders to refuse respectable colored persons seats, but had repeatedly remonstrated with his drivers, and the reason given by them was the same which your conductor gave—i. e. "the passengers make a fuss," &c.

You lay the blame on the universal, ubiquitous Public, whereas, Mr Public would have no more objection to riding with me in a Knickerbocker than in a Third avenue stage, and the same worthy gentleman could as easily distinguish my color (which is far from being white) in the Harlem as in the Twenty-seventh st cars.

I have long wished some of our liberal papers would notice the unjust proscription; and my object is to put the saddle on the right horse, and convince omnibus proprietors and railroad companies, that by abolishing such rules where they do exist they would make nine six pences where they would lose one. P. A. B.

New-York, September 9, 1850.

the treatment of the black woman was not the fault of the conductor or the streetcar company, but the "shameful" and "loathsome" general attitude in society toward black people. This attitude, he maintained, was left over from the days when slavery had been legal.

New York, the writer claimed, had fallen behind New England in addressing the issue of segregated transportation. "Africans are carried now the same as Whites throughout the greater part of New-England, though twenty years ago" it was "as brutal there as it now is here."

He accused white New Yorkers of being hypocrites. "Let us purify our own borders before arraying ourselves in a grand crusade against the sins of our neighbors" in the South, he wrote.

Several days later a man who identified himself only by the

initials P.A.B. wrote a letter in response. Because of the context of his letter, it's clear that he was black. Wanting to share his observations, he noted that from his experiences it was not the passengers but the conductors who were responsible.

"In nine cases out of ten the passengers have no objection," he wrote. "I can ride [without anyone objecting] in the Brooklyn omnibuses or in the cars of any Railroad except the City [Manhattan] cars. In the North River*, New-Haven, Harlem, Long Island, and all the Jersey lines I am a frequent passenger and I always take first class cars, and I have never yet been refused a passage, but on our City cars and omnibuses I am either rejected or pointed to an outside seat, which I of course refuse, preferring to walk. . . ."

Specifically, the letter writer stressed, the problem seemed to stem from individual conductors. He mentioned a conversation he'd had with the owner of an omnibus company who told him that he'd never given orders to refuse "respectable colored persons seats" but that his drivers often did so anyway, claiming, whether or not it was true, that "the passengers made a fuss."

It's clear that the issue of mistreatment of black riders on public transportation was not new in 1854 and had been much discussed and debated. What had happened to Elizabeth Jennings was another in a long line of incidents in which conductors insulted, pushed, and ejected black passengers.

* The North River is the old term for the lower part of the Hudson in the vicinity of New York City.

Trying to Make a Difference

Some white people in the North, upset by the treatment of black travelers, found small ways to show their support and fight for change.

The attorney David L. Child of Boston, Massachusetts, wrote, for example, about one small effort to pressure steamboat captains to treat black passengers fairly. Child, one of a group of eight white men who were delegates of the American Anti-Slavery Society, praised a white steamboat captain named Lewis Davis for his equitable treatment of black passengers. Child and his group had recently traveled together from Philadelphia to New York City partly on Captain Davis's boat.

By calling attention in the press to Captain Davis, whose steamboat, *Philadelphia*, carried passengers between Philadelphia and Bristol, Pennsylvania, Child hoped to inspire other captains to act in a more equitable manner toward black passengers.

Child noted that the delegates of the American Anti-Slavery Society were willing to boycott other more convenient ways of travel in order to support Captain Davis.

"All of the . . . gentlemen were desirous . . . to go by the Rail Road Line, via Bordentown and Amboy," wrote Child, "but they chose to take a circuitous," or roundabout, "route, and a slower way of getting to their destination. They did this to show their appreciation of the captain of a boat who treated white and black travelers as equals." Child added that Captain Davis's competitors had lost business worth about twenty-seven dollars, which was what the men's tickets cost.

Hoping that others would take note, Child publicized his account. His letter was published in the May 7, 1831, edition of *The Liberator*, where perhaps it inspired others to do the same.

William Lloyd Garrison and *The Liberator*

William Lloyd Garrison, founder of *The Liberator*.

"I am in earnest. I will not equivocate. I will not excuse. I will not retreat a single inch *and I will be heard.*" Those words were written by William Lloyd Garrison in the first issue of *The Liberator*, an antislavery newspaper he founded in Boston, Massachusetts, in 1831.

A white man raised in poverty in Newburyport, Massachusetts, Garrison became one of the most outspoken and passionate antislavery advocates in the United States. He didn't write only about slavery, however. He was vigilant in condemning the inequality that free blacks in the North were facing. One of the issues he was concerned about was segregation in northern modes of transportation.

A newspaper editor by training, Garrison had grown impatient with the antislavery movement while working for two years as an assistant to Benjamin Lundy, a New Jersey Quaker and an antislavery advocate. Garrison despised the idea of gradual emancipation, believing instead that slavery should end everywhere immediately, and he also found that Lundy's writings on the topic were too mild.

By launching *The Liberator*, Garrison altered the tone of the antislavery movement. In 1832 he started the New England Antislavery Society and, the following year, helped found the American Anti-Slavery Society.

Garrison received countless death threats but remained undeterred. He died in 1879 at the age of seventy-four.

Horace Greeley and the *New-York Daily Tribune*

Among large American newspapers, the *New-York Daily Tribune* was far from typical. The newspaper reflected the progressive outlook of its publisher and editor, a white man named Horace Greeley. He was born into a poor family in New Hampshire in 1811.

Greeley was a man with an opinion about almost everything, from vegetarianism (he was in favor of it) to alcohol (he was against it). He was well known for his strong antislavery views. He is said to have helped Abraham Lincoln get elected and afterward leaned on the president to declare the emancipation of enslaved people.

Disturbed by the influence of what was called the gutter press, which was a type of newspaper that focused only on sensational and outrageous stories, Greeley started the *New-York Daily Tribune* as an alternative. His newspaper was a success, becoming the largest in New York and perhaps all of America. Weekly editions were mailed to subscribers around the country. When Elizabeth Jennings was injured and ejected from the streetcar, the *New-York Daily Tribune* published her firsthand account on July 19, 1854, bringing the story to a wide audience that reached far beyond New York.

Horace Greeley, founder of the *New-York Daily Tribune*.

Another focal point for Greeley was the American West. He became famous for the iconic phrase *Go west, young man*, although he may not have been the first to use it. The town (now city) of Greeley, Colorado, was named after him.

Greeley tried his hand at politics, serving a short vacancy for a congressman who had resigned. He ran an unsuccessful campaign for president in 1872 and, in failing mental and physical health, unsuccessfully attempted to return to journalism. He died on November 29, 1872.

Chester A. Arthur in a picture taken around 1858.

EIGHT

A Future U.S. President

A VOLUNTEER at the First Colored American Congregational Church passed the hat that night from row to row, and people gave what they could afford to help the Jennings family pay for an attorney.

The black community was behind Elizabeth. But could a lawyer be found who would take the case?

It was a long shot. With very few exceptions lawyers were white men. It would be difficult to find one interested in taking on an equal rights case involving a black woman.

With few places to turn, members of the committee that was formed at the church to advocate for Elizabeth visited the office of a lawyer named Erastus D. Culver, a well-known abolitionist. Culver was sympathetic. He was deeply disturbed by the story and agreed that it deserved to be heard in a court of law.

But Culver had to turn the committee down. A year before, in the spring of 1853, he had been elected as a city judge in Brooklyn. He had turned over all his cases to a young lawyer in his practice. In an interesting twist of history, the newly minted attorney was Chester A. Arthur, who would one day be the twenty-first president of the United States.

But that was far in the future. The committee members who met

The Fugitive Slave Act

New York City was growing rapidly. The population surged in 1855 to a new high of 629,810 because of immigration. Most of the newcomers were white and came from Ireland and Germany.

Meanwhile, the number of black residents of the city was on the decline, decreasing from 16,358 in 1840 to 13,815 in 1850. From 1850 to 1855 the black population dropped again, to 11,740.

The decline was caused in large part by the fact that blacks in New York City, as well as other northern cities, were increasingly in danger, and even more so following the passage of the Fugitive Slave Act.

Signed into law in 1850 by President Millard Fillmore, the Fugitive Slave Act meant that runaway slaves who fled to the North could be captured and returned to the South. This included even those who had lived as free men and women in the North for decades.

Slave catchers were already doing a brisk business in New York, where runaway slaves could be found quickly because there were more leads in populated areas. Many blacks left the city and headed to farms or small towns in the countryside, where they hoped they would be undetected. A large number of blacks left the United States altogether and settled in Canada.

The new law instantly transformed free states such as New York from places where a runaway slave could count on a certain level of opportunity and safety to places where southern laws about slavery were enforced. Some historians believe that the passage and signing of the Fugitive Slave Act led America into the Civil War.

The new law also harshly punished those who helped to protect runaway slaves. New Yorkers played a major role in the Underground Railroad, a network of hidden routes and secret hideaways where escaped slaves received help on their journeys to freedom. Now sheltering fugitive slaves or simply interfering with their recapture put these antislavery volunteers in danger.

While there had long been the possibility that any black person, whether a fugitive or not, could be kidnapped, taken south, and sold to a slave owner, the new law made that scenario much more likely. Even someone like Elizabeth Jennings, born free in a northern state, faced this risk. Sometimes it was a case of mistaken identity. In other cases bounty hunters, motivated by greed, kidnapped the first black persons they encountered. Once they were in the South, there was little that could be done, although there were some cases in which money was raised and a kidnapped person's freedom was purchased.

The officer of Justice! arresting a helpless female fugitive in N. Y.
What has the North to do with Slavery?

The capture of a black female fugitive in New York.

Chester Arthur that day in 1854 were surely disappointed that they wouldn't be able to hire Erastus Culver and were being asked to accept an attorney who was just twenty-four years old and who had been a lawyer officially for exactly six weeks.

Yet Chester Arthur was impressive in his own right. He had earned the respect of Erastus Culver in a very short time. Chester had been an apprentice to Culver for the previous year, and Culver certified to the Supreme Court of New York that the young man was "of good moral character," an endorsement that is still required (though described differently from state to state) before someone is allowed to practice law. Culver was so enthusiastic, in fact, that even before Chester Arthur was granted official permission to practice law, he'd been made a partner in the renamed law firm of Culver, Parker and Arthur.

Erastus Culver must have been very persuasive to convince the committee members that Chester Arthur could handle Elizabeth

Chester A. Arthur: His Early Years

Chester A. Arthur was the fifth child in a poor white family that had strong antislavery views. His father, a Baptist minister named William Arthur, preached about the evils of slavery from the church pulpit.

William Arthur, who was born in the township of Dreen, County Antrim, Ireland, was so fiercely opposed to slavery that it led to problems in his career. Parishioners of a church he served in Greenwich, New York, from 1839 to 1844, for example, reported that he gave so many sermons on the topic that they grew tired of him.

He and his wife, a Vermont native named Malvina Stone, and their children relocated eleven times as he served churches in Vermont, western New York State, and the area surrounding Albany, New York, the state capital.

Chester A. Arthur was born while the family lived in Franklin County, Vermont. He was born on October 5, 1830, though some historians believe that it was a year earlier. (Some historians have also argued that Chester Arthur was actually born across the border in Canada. This would become an issue for him when he ran for national office because being born outside the United States would have disqualified him.)

In 1844 the family was relocated to the Albany, New York, area so that Elder Arthur, as Chester Arthur's father was called, could serve as pastor of the First Particular Baptist Church

Jennings's case. Arthur was very young, it was true, but he was extremely bright and hardworking. Culver won them over.

What the committee members didn't know, but would soon learn, was that Chester Arthur was as passionate about the rights of blacks as was Erastus Culver.

Still, the young attorney admitted privately that he was overwhelmed. He had little time for anything but work and rarely left the office, at 289 Broadway, or his room at a nearby boardinghouse.

Although he told friends he missed having a social life, he recognized that Culver's faith in him presented a great opportunity that should not be wasted.

"It comes rather hard at first," he wrote to his mother, "but it will do me a great deal of good."

He had been given a chance to prove himself. But was he up to the challenge?

and Society of Gibbonsville and West Troy. At last Elder Arthur had found a place where he was welcome. He became friendly with the faculty of Union College, including its nationally known president, Eliphalet Nott. The college in 1845 awarded Elder Arthur an honorary master of arts degree, coinciding with his work as editor of *The Antiquarian and General Review*, a magazine of "popular knowledge, covering history, philology, religion, and science."

Young Chester was enrolled at Union College in September 1845. Often described as "amiable," or friendly, Chester was well liked but not a great student. One teacher recalled that he was "frank and open in his manners, and genial in his disposition."

For most of his college career Chester Arthur seemed more interested in having a good time than following in the footsteps of his serious-minded father. He was known to get into trouble for silly pranks, such as carving his name into wooden objects around campus or throwing the college bell into the Erie Canal. Having studied the French language and Greek and Latin philosophers, among other subjects, he was graduated from Union College in July 1848.

Chester Arthur did have one moment before he left Union College that revealed a serious side to him that would become more apparent when he went on to study law. He wrote an essay in which he argued that slavery infected the very soul of the nation itself.

THE BROOKLYN CITY HALL.

Brooklyn City Hall (now Borough Hall), where the case of *Elizabeth Jennings v. Third Avenue Railroad Company* was heard.

NINE

▬

Elizabeth Jennings v. Third Avenue Railroad Company

CHESTER ARTHUR WASTED NO TIME. Working closely with Elizabeth Jennings and her supporters, he filed a lawsuit in the Supreme Court of the State of New York. The lawsuit sought damages(payment) from the streetcar company, the conductor, and the driver of the team of horses (but not the police officer, who was not named in the lawsuit). They would have to pay a certain amount of money, to be decided in court, to Elizabeth Jennings if they lost.

Although the assault had taken place in Manhattan, the lawsuit was filed in Brooklyn because the company that owned the streetcar line, the Third Avenue Railroad Company, had its headquarters there.

One might wonder why Chester Arthur didn't pursue a *criminal* case, in which those guilty of assaulting Elizabeth Jennings could have gone to jail if convicted. The answer comes from Elizabeth's father.

What they really wanted, Thomas Jennings wrote, was to change the system.

Winning a criminal case would punish a small number of people, the men who assaulted Elizabeth. Winning a civil case, however, could improve the lives of all black New Yorkers, in the present and in the future. The owners of the streetcar company, if forced to pay Elizabeth

Jennings damages in a civil suit, might end segregation on their streetcars rather than risk further costly lawsuits from others.

What Elizabeth Jennings and her father were trying to do was force the issue so that all blacks, regardless of who they were, would be able to ride with respect and dignity on New York City streetcars.

It was a wise and calculated move, which Thomas Jennings explained in a letter to Elizabeth's supporters.

"Now, I am not aware of any difference in the law of this state in relation to persons of color . . ." he wrote. "What we want to know is what our legal rights are in this matter, not by hearsay, but by the decision of the Supreme Court of the State of New York." Referring to the attack on his daughter, he added, "The assault, though a very aggravated case, is only secondary in our view to the rights of our people."

Chester Arthur listened to this reasoning and agreed that it was the best path to victory.

Now, with the filing of the lawsuit done, they would have to be patient. There was no guarantee that the suit would move forward. A judge could review the lawsuit, find that it held no merit under the law, and decide that it would not be heard, or have its day in court.

After a few months, though, there was good news: the lawsuit could go forward.

The conductor, identified only by his last name, Moss, and the driver, whose name we don't know, chose not to fight the lawsuit, meaning they would accept the court's decision.

The streetcar company, however, began preparing for battle. The case of *Elizabeth Jennings v. Third Avenue Railroad Company* was headed to court.

FEBRUARY 22, 1855, the day of the trial, was a brutally cold day in an unusually frigid month. Seven months had passed since the hot July afternoon when Elizabeth Jennings was assaulted.

The morning started early for Elizabeth, her parents, and Chester

Arthur. They had to travel to Brooklyn; that meant crossing the icy East River from Manhattan.

The New York State Supreme Court, Second Judicial District, was located within Brooklyn's City Hall, now Borough Hall, which had been built in 1848. Four judges traveled throughout the district, which included Kings County, Brooklyn. Among them was a man named William Rockwell who would preside over Elizabeth's case.

Despite severely cold weather, the courtroom was "crowded almost to suffocation," according to one account. Those in attendance likely included members of the First Colored American Congregational Church in Manhattan as well as other black churches and civic organizations in Manhattan and perhaps also Brooklyn. At least one reporter, from *The Brooklyn Daily Eagle*, was present.

Details of the testimony have been lost to time, probably in a 1911 fire at the state library in Albany. However, among the important witnesses was almost certainly Sarah E. Adams, Elizabeth's friend and companion. Others probably included the German man who had written down his name and address and given it to Elizabeth and Elizabeth's father, Thomas Jennings, who could have testified about his daughter's injuries that he had observed after she limped home.

And while it's not known for sure, it's very likely that Elizabeth Jennings herself was the star witness. Because her father had wisely asked her to write down a firsthand account immediately, Elizabeth would have been able to provide excellent testimony. She would not have had to rely on her memory seven months after the event.

While Elizabeth Jennings was permitted to be a plaintiff—a person who takes another to court—the judicial system was unfair to people of color. Elizabeth Jennings faced a jury made up of white men. The judge and all the attorneys involved in the case were white men, too. Was fairness even possible?

The lawyers defending the Third Avenue Railroad Company had several options. They might have argued that the company owners couldn't be held

Illustration from a Boston newspaper shows people crossing the frozen East River from Brooklyn to New York (Manhattan).

Getting to Brooklyn

How did Elizabeth Jennings, her parents, and her attorney, Chester Arthur, get from Manhattan to Brooklyn on the morning her case was heard in court on February 22, 1855?

It's possible they had to walk across a nearly frozen East River. While small boats and ferries routinely transported passengers between Manhattan and Brooklyn, occasionally the river was clogged with blocks of ice. On Elizabeth Jennings's court date the weather was unusually bitter, as it had been all month. They either trekked across the river or they had a very cold ride on a small boat whose captain had to dodge large chunks of ice.

Why didn't they just cross over the famous Brooklyn Bridge? It wasn't completed until 1883, almost thirty years in the future.

responsible for the actions of the company employees. They might have tried to persuade the jury that the company's employees had the right to keep Elizabeth Jennings off the streetcar by claiming that as the owners of a private company they could operate as they chose. They probably tried to undermine Elizabeth Jennings and her witnesses or to insist that she hadn't been hurt as badly as she claimed.

After closing arguments Judge Rockwell spoke to the jury (this is known as charging, or instructing the jury). He told the jurors that under the law in his jurisdiction, a company was indeed liable (held responsible) for the actions of its employees. It made no difference, he said, whether an employee did something on purpose and with intent or was simply careless.

He added that streetcar companies, although private, were in the business of serving the public. Thus they must, he said, "carry all respectable persons."

He went on to point to a state statute—in other words, a law previously passed—that stated, "Colored persons, if sober, well-behaved, and free from disease, [have] the same rights as others." They could not be excluded, he noted, by any rules governing the company. They could not be treated with force or violence. And if they were excluded or expelled from a streetcar, the company could be held responsible.

The judge's instructions were very clear. A law that already existed in New York State supported Elizabeth Jennings and her position. In making a decision, the jurors needed to answer just one question: Did they believe Elizabeth and her witnesses?

A lawyer makes his case in this engraving of a courtroom scene from the 1800s.

TEN

—

The Jury's Decision

ALL THEY COULD DO WAS WAIT.

Chester Arthur, Thomas Jennings, and of course Elizabeth Jennings herself would have been very apprehensive. They had planned for this moment and cared deeply about the outcome—not just for Elizabeth's sake but for all black New Yorkers. But would the jurors, now deliberating privately in another room, take her side? Or would they do what jurors often did and fail to find justice for a black person?

No one can predict a jury's decision. Composed of a group of ordinary people, local and state juries are often made up of between six and twelve members, depending on the rules of the individual court. Under oath and in secrecy, the jury discusses the facts of a case and decides the outcome based on the evidence and the law.

When the jury filed back into the courtroom, it meant a decision had been made. The head juror, selected by the others, was told to approach the bench and hand a slip of paper to the judge.

Judge Rockwell unfolded the paper. He read it and spoke. "The jury has awarded Miss Jennings $225 plus 10 percent for court costs," he said.

She had won!

Chester Arthur had asked for the huge sum of five hundred dollars, but the amount she was awarded was still very surprising. Today, because of inflation, it would be close to six thousand dollars.

However, it was the exact words of Judge Rockwell, preserved forever in newspaper accounts, that mattered most to Elizabeth Jennings and her supporters. The strategy of Thomas Jennings and the church committee, carried out by Chester Arthur, had worked. The clear winners were the black residents of New York.

Judge Rockwell in his instructions had delivered words of justice long denied. By siding with Elizabeth Jennings, the jury confirmed the judge's words.

"The streetcar companies must 'carry all respectable persons.' "

"Colored persons [have] the same rights as others."

Newspapers far and wide carried the story. A WHOLESOME VERDICT, reported the *New-York Daily Tribune*.

RIGHTS OF COLOURED PEOPLE VINDICATED, the *National Anti-Slavery Standard*'s headline all but shouted to the world.

LEGAL RIGHTS VINDICATED, Frederick Douglass declared in *Frederick Douglass' Paper*.

This was a victory to be celebrated! The black community of New York, and beyond, was overjoyed. Whites who supported black equality were thrilled. The court victory was a boost in morale and a message of hope at a time when they were needed badly.

Elizabeth Jennings had arrived in court that morning knowing the odds were against her. She left a hero. As she made her way back to Manhattan, possibly walking across the ice-covered East River, perhaps she saw the city, her city, as a changed place, and in fact it was. From that moment on she had the right to ride on any streetcar she wanted. And so did everyone else.

The owners of the Third Avenue Railroad Company did not contest the decision but moved quickly to integrate their cars. Other streetcar companies soon followed their lead. The company owners understood that if they didn't put a stop to segregation on their streetcars, there

Some of the newspapers that published the jury's
decision. The *Anti-Slavery Bugle*, published in Ohio,
was one of several newspapers that reprinted the
original story from the *National Anti-Slavery Standard*.

RIGHTS OF COLORED PEOPLE VINDICATED.

The hardships and insults so long suffered by the colored people of this city, in consequence of the general refusal of omnibus and railroad proprietors to permit them to enjoy equal rights as passengers, are, we hope, nearly at an end; the Supreme Court (Brooklyn Circuit, Judge Rockwell presiding) having made a decision which places that class of our citizens upon an equality with all others. The decision referred to was made in the case of Elizabeth Jennings vs. the Third Avenue Railroad Company. The circumstances attending the expulsion of Miss Jennings from one of the cars of that company, last Summer, as published in the STANDARD at the time of their occurrence, were briefly these, viz.: Miss Jennings who is a teacher in one of the public schools, and organist in one of the colored churches, got upon one of the Company's cars on the Sabbath, to ride to church. The conductor finally undertook to get her off, first alleging the car was full; and when that was shown to be false, he pretended the other passengers were displeased at her presence; but she saw nothing of that, and insisted on her rights, he took hold of her by force to expel her. She resisted, they got her down on the platform, jammed her bonnet, soiled her dress, and injured her person. Quite a crowd gathered around, but she effectually resisted, and they were not able to get her off. Finally, after the car had gone on further, they got the aid of a policeman, and succeeded in getting her from the car. She instructed her attorneys, Messrs. Culver, Parker and Arthur, to prosecute the Company, together with the driver and conductor. The two latter interposed no defence, the Company took issue, and the cause was brought to trial on the 22d ult. Judge Rockwell gave a very clear and able charge, instructing the Jury that the Company were liable for the acts of their agents, whether committed carelessly and negligently or wilfully and maliciously; that they were common carriers, and as such bound to carry all respectable persons: *that colored persons, if sober, well behaved, and free from disease, had the same rights as others; and could neither be excluded by any rules of the Company nor by force or violence;* and in case of such expulsion or exclusion, the Company was liable.

The plaintiff claimed $500 in her complaint, and a majority of the Jury were for giving her the full amount; but others maintained some peculiar notions as to colored people's rights, and they finally agreed on $225, on which the Court added ten per cent. besides the costs.

COURT RECORD.

Circuit Court.
BEFORE JUDGE ROCKWELL.

February 22.

Elizabeth Jennings vs. The Third avenue Railroad Company.—The plaintiff is a colored lady, a teacher in one of the public schools, and the organist in one of the churches in New York. She got upon one of the Company's cars last summer, on the Sabbath, to ride to church. The conductor finally undertook to get her off, first alleging the car was full, and when that was shown to be untrue, he pretended the other passengers were displeased at her presence; but as she saw nothing of that, and insisted on her rights, he took hold of her by force to expel her. She resisted, they got her down on the platform, jammed her bonnet soiled her dress, and injured her person. Quite a crowd gathered around, but she effectually resisted, and they were not able to get her off. Finally, after the car had gone on further, they got the aid of a policeman, and succeeded in getting her from the car. She instructed her attorneys, Messrs. Culver, Parker and Arthur, to prosecute the Company, together with the driver and conductor. The two latter interposed no defence, the Company took issue, and the cause was yesterday brought to trial. Judge Rockwell charged, instructing the Jury that the Company were liable for the acts of their agents, whether committed carelessly and negligently, or wilfully and maliciously. That they were common carriers, and as such bound to carry all respectable persons; that colored persons, if sober, well-behaved, and free from disease, had the same rights as others; and could neither be excluded by any rules of the Company, nor by force or violence; and in case of such expulsion or exclusion, the Company was liable.

The plaintiff claimed $500 in her complaint; and the Jury agreed on $225, on which the Court added ten per cent. besides the costs.

Newspaper coverage of the jury's decision. On this page, from left to right: *National Anti-Slavery Standard* (here, reprinted with a slightly different headline in the *Anti-Slavery Bugle*) and the *Brooklyn Daily Eagle*. Opposite page: The *Pacific Appeal* published an entire overview of the case, including an announcement of the verdict reprinted from the *New-York Daily Tribune*, in a retrospective published several years later.

A WHOLESALE VERDICT.—The case of Elizabeth Jennings *vs.* the Third Avenue Railroad Company, was tried yesterday in the Brooklin Circuit Court, before Judge Rockwell. The plaintiff is a colored lady, a teacher in one of the public schools, and the organist in one of the churches in this City. She got upon one of the Company's cars last summer, on the Sabbath, to ride to church. The conductor finally undertook to get her off, first alleging the car was full, and when that was shown to be false, he pretended the other passengers were displeased at her presence; but as she saw nothing of that, and insisted on her rights, he took hold of her by force to expel her. She resisted; they got her down on the platform, jammed her bonnet, soiled her dress, and injured her person. Quite a crowd gathered around, but she effectually resisted, and they were not able to get her off Finally, after the car had gone on further, they got the aid of a policeman, and succeeded in getting her from the car. She instructed her attorneys, Messrs. Culver. Parker and Arthur, to prosecute the Company, together with the driver and conductor. The two latter interposed no defence, the company took issue, and the cause was yesteaday brought to trial. Judge Rockwell gave a very clear and able charge, instructing the jury that the Company were liable for the acts of their agents, whether committed carelessly and negligently or wilfully and maliciously. That they were common carriers, and as such bound to carry all respectable persons; *that colored persons, if sober, well-behaved and free from disease,* had the same rights as others; and could neither be excluded by *any rules of the Company, nor by force or violence;* and in case of such expulsion or exclusion, the Company was liable.

The plaintiff claimed $500 in her complaint, and a majority of the jury were for giving her the full amount; but others maintained some peculiar notions as to colored people's rights, and they finally agreed on $225, on which the court added ten per cent., besides the costs.

Railroads, steamboats, omnibusses and ferry-boats, will be admonished from this, as to the rights of respectable colored people. It is high time the rights of this class of citizens were ascertained, and that it should be known whether they are to be thrust from our public conveyances, while women, with a quarter of mutton or a load of codfish, can be admitted would be more incidents, and they would face similar lawsuits, which they would almost certainly lose, now that the court had sided with Elizabeth Jennings.

In fact other segregated systems of transportation in New York City were affected by the ruling, too. "Railroads, steamboats, omnibuses, and ferry boats will be admonished* from this, as to the rights of respectable colored people," the *New-York Daily Tribune* reported.

Progress is often accompanied by steps backward, so it's not surprising that several incidents in which black riders encountered discrimination on the city's streetcars were reported during the next two years. A few conductors still tried to discriminate against black riders. The official end to discrimination in transportation in New York City occurred with the passage of the New York State Civil Rights Act of 1873.

But Elizabeth Jennings's success in court is considered by historians to be the first major breakthrough of its kind in New York.

The case had another positive result: Thomas Jennings was inspired to launch the Legal Rights Association, which would help black New Yorkers find and pay for attorneys to represent them in future cases.

As for Elizabeth, the court case catapulted her from an admired young teacher to a hero in the pursuit of equal rights for blacks. Black New Yorkers celebrated the anniversary of her court victory for years. In so doing, they honored a remarkable woman, who, on her way to choir practice one Sunday afternoon, rose up against racism and won.

Footnote: warned

PART II

A FORGOTTEN HERO

Rosa Parks in Montgomery, Alabama, on December 1, 1955.

ELEVEN

An Uncanny Similarity to Rosa Parks

ONE HUNDRED YEARS AFTER ELIZABETH JENNINGS had her day in court, a forty-two-year-old black seamstress named Rosa Parks was removed from a segregated bus and arrested in Montgomery, Alabama. Mrs. Parks had refused to comply with a law that required her to move back from the first row of the "Colored" section when the area designated for whites was filled with passengers.

That incident, which occurred on December 1, 1955, was carefully and thoughtfully anticipated by Mrs. Parks and the National Association for the Advancement of Colored People (NAACP). Her actions spurred on the Montgomery bus boycott and were an important step toward ending segregation in Montgomery's public transportation system, just as the Elizabeth Jennings case was in New York City.

Mrs. Parks would prove to be an enduring figure. Her dignity and courage would resonate throughout the world.

Rosa Parks became a legend.

Elizabeth Jennings was largely forgotten.

Why?

There may be several reasons. Elizabeth Jennings lived in an era before modern media. When Mrs. Parks made her heroic stand, the story

New-York Daily Tribune.
Vᵒ XIV...Nᵒ 4,139.   NEW-YORK, TUESDAY, JULY 18, 1854.   PRICE TWO CENTS.

New-York Daily Tribune.
Vᵒ XIV. Nᵒ 4,124.   NEW-YORK, WEDNESDAY, JULY 19, 1854.   PRICE TWO CENTS.

WILL KANSAS BE A FREE OR SLAVE STATE!

A Joint Stock Society with a large capital has been established for the purpose of encouraging immigration into Kansas, and the abolitionists are straining every nerve to persuade the people to go into that country for the purpose of preventing its preoccupation by slaveholders. On the other hand, the citizens of Missouri are carrying their property into the disputed territory, thus vindicating their equal right to go into any portion of a common country without the injustice of expulsion or confiscation. The abolition journals attach great consequence to this contest; we attach none whatsoever. The introduction of Slavery into the new Territory would not add one slave to the aggregate slave population. It would not strengthen the institution or its interests. We have seen an argument that slaves would increase more rapidly in a fresh and fertile country. Those who will look at the extensive area of the southern States, at its cheap lands and unlimited abundance, will readily see that the increase of Slavery is not limited by any want of subsistence or employment. There is enough of land and labor to employ all the southern slaves, even if they do not go to Kansas. But the theories of political philosophers are rarely realized by events. The geographical position of Kansas is such that its nearest outlets must be through southern States, and by way of southern ports. Its cotton, hemp and tobacco whether grown by free or slave labor, will thus tend to promote the commercial prosperity of the South. The great railroad to the Pacific will pass near Kansas. The interests of that State will be thus united with the southern States, in spite of the malevolent motives with which it is now sought to be settled with the sworn foes of the South. Let the Abolitionists organize immigrant companies; let them administer the Anti-Slavery oaths to them. The first crop made in Kansas will be sent by a southern route—will be sold in a southern port, and the immigrant will perceive the selfish injustice by which he was sent as the irreconcilable foe of those with whom his interests are identical. For these reasons we feel no anxiety as to the institutions of Kansas. Slavery is stronger at home than when diffused by propagandism. States located within the cotton and sugar latitude, can never be persuaded to war against those great staples. And the time will come when any injury to Charleston, Norfolk, Baltimore or New-Orleans will be resisted with as much courage by Kansas and Nebraska, as the invasion of those cities was, during the last war, by the people of Ohio, Illinois, and Indiana. Since the sectional line has been obliterated, and the badge of disqualification removed, we are indifferent whether the country shall be dedicated to Slavery or not. God and geography have given the commercial control of the new territory to the southern States, and all the British Abolitionists in New-York and Canada, cannot deprive us of it.

[Baltimore Patriot.]

was covered by daily newspapers, wire service reporters, photographers, radio, and television. Within a few hours Rosa Parks's story and photo were distributed far and wide.

Mrs. Parks also had the support and backing of the NAACP, which did not exist in the 1850s.

For its time the Elizabeth Jennings case was a significant story that received national attention through the writings of Frederick Douglass as well as Horace Greeley's *New-York Daily Tribune*. The majority of newspapers in the United States, however, were focused on a more pressing issue, slavery. Would it continue in the South? Would the institution be kept out of Kansas? Was a civil war over the issue unavoidable?

During the same week Elizabeth Jennings was assaulted in New York for standing up for equal treatment, advertisements in southern newspapers offered slaves for sale and rewards for escaped slaves. In Louisiana a slave owner offered ten dollars for the capture and return of "Charles," described as a "dark mulatto . . . about 13 years of age; 4 feet 3 to 5 inches high" and possibly heading to Mobile, Alabama, adding that he might have been trying to find his sister. Another advertisement offered for sale an entire group of slaves "consisting of Men, Women and Children," with payment requested in cash.

At far left, advertisements in a Louisiana newspaper in which slaves were offered for sale and rewards were posted for escaped slaves. The ads were reprinted with scathing commentary in the *New-York Daily Tribune*. At near left, an article in the next day's edition of the *Tribune*, "Will Kansas be a Free or Slave State?"

Nearly four million black men, women, and children were enslaved in the South at the start of the Civil War in 1861. The rights of free black people in the North, estimated at about 226,000, were also a vital cause but may have seemed less urgent.

The newspapers that did cover the Elizabeth Jennings story as it was unfolding in 1854 and 1855 went out of business long ago. Historical copies, if they survive at all, are mostly stored at research institutions.

At the time I started researching this story, the only way to find these newspaper accounts was to scroll through old microfilm, microfiche, and dusty volumes of archived papers at libraries and historical institutions. Some of these sources are now available on the internet, but certainly not all of them.

The fact that Elizabeth Jennings is a common name very likely contributed to her story's near disappearance. A popular name makes research more difficult. Elizabeth Jennings shares her name with countless people around the world, including an English poet who died in 2001.

Additionally, it seems possible that the assault and court case faded from the news because Elizabeth Jennings herself did little to keep the story alive. Perhaps she wanted to forget about the experience, or maybe she simply wanted to get back to doing what she loved most, which was teaching.

Sometimes it is difficult to explain why one person becomes famous while others simply vanish from history. This is part of what makes history so fascinating. There are always new stories to be discovered.

At other times a story is untold for what turns out to be a very specific reason. That is what happened to Claudette Colvin, a teenager who took a stand on a segregated bus in Montgomery, Alabama, on March 2, 1955, nine months prior to Rosa Parks. The city's black leaders felt that Claudette Colvin was an unfit role model and chose Mrs. Parks instead. When Phillip Hoose wrote *Claudette Colvin: Twice*

Toward Justice, readers finally learned about her courage and the significant case in which she testified.

In the case of Elizabeth Jennings, more than 160 years have passed since she stood up for her rights on a New York City streetcar. One wonders what she would think about her story being told now. How would she tell her story if she could tell it herself? Fortunately we know the answer, at least partially, to that question. Because she wrote down an account of the events of July 16, 1854, her words live on. In a sense, within the pages of this book, she has spoken for herself.

THE RIOTS IN NEW YORK : DESTRUCTION OF THE COLOURED ORPHAN ASYLUM.

Burning of the Colored Orphan Asylum during
the Draft Riots of 1863. Illustration courtesy of the
New-York Historical Society.

TWELVE

—

What Happened to Elizabeth Jennings?

Eʟɪᴢᴀʙᴇᴛʜ Jᴇɴɴɪɴɢꜱ ᴡᴀꜱ ᴀ ʜᴇʀᴏ in the eyes of the black community as well as white supporters of equal rights for blacks, but there were hard times ahead.

In 1859, four years after her victory in court, her beloved father died at the age of sixty-eight. He did not live to see the election of Abraham Lincoln, the Civil War, or the end of slavery in the United States.

A year after Thomas Jennings died, Elizabeth married a man named Charles Graham, a native of St. Croix, one of three islands that today constitute the U.S. Virgin Islands. Two years after they married, Elizabeth and Charles were blessed with the birth of a baby boy. He was named Thomas after Elizabeth's father.

But Thomas, when only a year old, became ill and died, an all-too-common fate for infants and children at the time. His death happened, by coincidence, during the Civil War draft riots, when horrible violence rocked Manhattan from July 13 through July 16, 1863. Much of the brutality was aimed at black bystanders. Elizabeth and Charles took a considerable risk when they insisted on escorting Thomas's body to Brooklyn for burial.

The riots were so vicious that many black residents fled the city as

The Civil War Draft Riots

The greatest crisis in U.S. history, the Civil War, which pitted the South and the North against each other, raised hopes among blacks that slavery in the South might end at last.

When the first shots were fired in 1861, many Americans assumed the war would end quickly. Instead, the war would last four years and cost an estimated 750,000 lives.

President Lincoln's signing in 1863 of the Emancipation Proclamation, which freed slaves in states that were in rebellion, was a day of great joy to those opposed to "the evil institution," as slavery was sometimes called. In reality, it took the victory of the North's Union army in 1865 and the passage of the Thirteenth Amendment for all the slaves to be freed.

Not everyone in the North was pleased with the prospect of millions of blacks suddenly being set free. Working-class whites, assuming that many of the former slaves would head north, were worried about losing their jobs.

With the help of antiwar newspapers, politicians opposed to Lincoln had been fanning the flames of anxiety among the white working class since Abraham Lincoln was elected president in 1860. By the time Lincoln signed the Emancipation Proclamation, many white workers were in a state of panic.

In New York City a tipping point occurred after a change in the federal draft law, which dictated the rules for required military service. The law was seen as unfair to poor

---

soon as they could. Elizabeth Jennings, her husband, and her mother were among them. They moved to Monmouth County, New Jersey, at the seashore, to live with Elizabeth's sister Matilda.

In 1867 Elizabeth's husband died. Charles Graham was just thirty-four years old. He and Elizabeth had been married for seven years. They'd had no more children after Thomas.

Elizabeth, her sister Matilda, and their mother continued to live at the New Jersey seashore, in or near Eatontown, New Jersey, for several more years. In 1871, they returned to Manhattan, where they resided at 543 Broome Street, and Elizabeth began working as a teacher at the 41st Street School.

and working-class people. Men who could pay three hundred dollars (a very large sum at the time) could avoid being drafted.

In the early morning of July 13, 1863, on the west side of Manhattan along Eighth and Ninth avenues, the riots began. At first the white rioters, many of whom were Irish immigrants, vented their rage on military and government buildings. Within a few hours, however, rioters began to focus their anger on any black person they encountered.

During five days of rioting, countless black men, women, and children were injured. Eleven black men were lynched. Black-owned businesses were torched. The Colored Orphan Asylum at Fifth Avenue and Forty-third Street was ransacked by a mob of several thousand men and women. Amazingly, all the children were evacuated before the building was burned to the ground.

White people who tried to intervene were also attacked. Rioters destroyed the property of a few whites who were known to be sympathetic to blacks, including the daughter of a well-known abolitionist and two women who were married to black men.

By the end of the rioting 119 people were verified as having been killed. It is one of the largest single incidents of civil disorder in the history of the United States. In response to the riots the federal government did back down, reducing the number of men who were selected for the draft.

Freedman's Bank record filled out by a clerk but signed by Elizabeth Jennings (Graham) at the bottom.

Two years later, in 1873, Elizabeth's mother died. Elizabeth found comfort and meaning in her work. She found a new place to live, a house at 237 West Forty-first Street. She continued to teach children for the rest of her life.

On April 5, 1895, along with two other black women, she opened, in her home on West Forty-first Street, a groundbreaking school, the first free kindergarten for black children in New York City. At the same time, and also in her home, she started a small but formal lending library. She stocked it with classic works of literature and loaned the books for free to people in her neighborhood.

The same woman who had made the first major breakthrough in ending

The First Free Kindergarten for Colored Children in New York City

When Elizabeth Jennings (under her married name Elizabeth J. Graham) started a kindergarten in her home with two other black women, Mrs. James Herbert Morse and Mrs. Edward Curtis, she was participating in a social movement in education that was considered cutting edge.

While we may take the idea of kindergarten for granted today, it was a startling idea when it was introduced in Germany in 1837 by a man named Friedrich Fröbel. He believed that playtime, if carefully supervised by teachers, was more important for young children than learning to read, write, and solve math problems. His idea was that games, songs, and activities would allow young children to mature and flourish.

Fröbel's idea caught on and spread to the United States. At first, kindergartens, where they existed, were private. New York and Boston took the lead on starting kindergartens that were free, allowing less fortunate children to enroll.

By starting a free kindergarten for black children—the first one in New York City—Elizabeth Jennings and her cofounders were pioneers in the battle for equal opportunity in education, a struggle that continues to this day in many parts of the United States.

A magazine article written by H. Cordelia Ray, one of ten black women chosen to serve on an executive committee to provide oversight of the kindergarten, provides a firsthand look. The school was financed by patrons (donors), Miss Ray wrote. While the race of the donors wasn't mentioned in the article, the context implies that they were most likely black.

An experienced kindergarten teacher named Leonie G. Rickard, who was probably the segregated streetcar system in New York remained dedicated to progress, justice, education, and equality. When she died in 1901 at the age of seventy-four, in an upstairs room while children played downstairs, it was the end of a life well lived. Elizabeth Jennings left behind an important legacy: she provided an example of how an individual person, if strong and determined, can make the world a better place, especially if she works toward a common goal with the help of a supportive community.

---

black, was hired to be in charge of the school. The number of students is not known.

Miss Ray's description of the kindergarten reveals her enthusiasm. "To visit the school-room is a delightful way to spend a morning. . . . Pretty pictures of flowers, fruit and child life adorn the walls; some of the work of the children is arranged for inspection, and everything around is bright and tasteful. . . . But by far the most attractive feature is in the little children themselves . . . who are either seated at their desks, engaged in some handiwork adapted to their tiny fingers, or playing one of their many beautiful games. It is stimulating to watch their artless enjoyment and graceful movements . . . while we realize that underneath the outer manifestations are the underlying principles being so unconsciously learned."

Miss Ray also mentioned the outdoor activities that were central to Fröbel's philosophy. "A yard connected with the house in which the school is situated has been carefully prepared, where the little ones have planted seeds and roots, and where they have an opportunity to exercise and play," Miss Ray wrote. "Thus a love of the beautiful will be instilled into these youthful minds in accordance with the idea of the great founder of the kindergarten system."

In addition to the kindergarten, two other programs sponsored by the same group were being held in the house, Miss Ray wrote. One was a sewing school on Saturday mornings for older pupils. The other was a small lending library. It was named by donors after the person who was serving as the librarian: Elizabeth Jennings Graham.

The house belonging to Chester A. Arthur in Ossining, New York.

THIRTEEN
—

How a Creepy Old House Led to the Writing of This Book

I LEARNED OF ELIZABETH JENNINGS because I was curious about an old, abandoned house.

From 1987 to 1996 my husband and I lived in Ossining, New York, a village on the Hudson River about an hour north of Manhattan. In our neighborhood there was a certain house, covered with vines and partially boarded up, that fascinated me. I could imagine that it had been very pretty at one time. Located across the street from a cemetery, the house was perched high on a hill and must have had beautiful views of the Hudson River.

A journalist is trained to keep her eyes open to possibilities. Who lived there? I wondered. Why does no one live there now? Why is it in such terrible shape? What will happen to it?

The neighborhood rumor (confirmed by a newspaper account and the local historical society) was that the house had once been the summer home of a New York lawyer named Chester A. Arthur. Yes, *that* Chester A. Arthur, the twenty-first president of the United States.

Now that got my attention.

I went to the library. The first thing I did was look up Chester A. Arthur, about whom I knew little. As I read about him, I was fascinated to learn that in his youth he had been a lawyer with a special interest in equal rights cases for blacks. There was a mention of a famous case he had won called *Elizabeth Jennings v. Third Avenue Railroad Company*. I had never heard of it.

I began to dig deeper. None of the old references spelled out the details of the case or, more important, answered the questions most urgently on my mind: who was Elizabeth Jennings, and what had happened?

Time and again, whenever the opportunity arose, I dug a little deeper. Researching Elizabeth Jennings became something of a hobby.

One Valentine's Day my husband asked me what I would like to do that day. What he meant was did I want to go out to dinner or maybe see a movie together. I told him that what I *really* wanted was to spend the day in New York City, preferably at the main branch of the New York Public Library, researching *Elizabeth Jennings v. Third Avenue Railroad Company*, and that he could go with me and it would be fun. And that's what we did.

These are the best kinds of mysteries. I found buried in the footnotes of old history books and on the pages of long-ago newspapers the hints of a story that sounded strangely similar to that of Rosa Parks, only it had taken place more than a hundred years earlier in New York City.

I turned to long-defunct newspapers and the writings of Frederick Douglass, all at the time on microfilm or microfiche, and learned that not only was Elizabeth Jennings a forgotten hero of equal rights for blacks but late in life she had been a founder of the first free black kindergarten in New York.

In the years since I began my research, her story, thanks to the internet, has begun to surface here and there. Much of the information about her, however, is brief, lacks context, and contains mistakes. This is one of the downsides of the internet: people copy and paste information without checking to see if it is correct. A lot of what is on the internet is wrong or misleading. Go to research libraries, small historical societies, and cemeteries, and find out the truth for yourself!

Meanwhile, Elizabeth Jennings's name also began to appear in academic books, a few museum exhibits, and at least one walking tour of New York. To the general public, however, Elizabeth Jennings is still mostly unknown.

Street sign, Elizabeth Jennings Place, added in 2007 in Manhattan near the actual site of the incident.

FOURTEEN

Retracing Her Footsteps

THE INTERSECTION WAS QUIET, almost peaceful, by the standards of
Manhattan.

Weirdly deserted, I thought.

This was the first time I had visited. It was September 2003,
and the spot where Elizabeth Jennings had boarded the streetcar and
been removed from it was not the busy intersection it had been in
1854. It was simply a place where two narrow and crooked streets
converged.

Although the spot was surrounded by enormous buildings, there
were no people in sight and no activity except for a discarded fast-food
wrapper caught by an occasional breeze.

As I studied the area, maps and notebooks in hand, I realized that I
was being watched by a police officer. The neighborhood is dominated
by court and police buildings, including the Metropolitan Correctional
Center, the U.S. District Court for the Southern District of New York,
the New York State Supreme Court, and the headquarters of the New
York City police department. It was just two years since the twin towers
of the World Trade Center, a short distance away, had been destroyed
by terrorists, resulting in the deaths of nearly three thousand people.

New York City was still on edge. As I juggled an armful of maps, both old and new, I found the towers' absence disorienting. I kept looking up, expecting them to be there.

I heard drumming, and, walking toward it, came across a civil rights march taking place at City Hall Park. A woman carried a placard that declared, Immigrant Women's Freedom March while another proclaimed, We Demand Civil Rights for All. Following them was a group carrying a sign, The Arab-American Family Support Center. And bringing up the rear was a group representing the hotel workers' union in New York.

Returning to the exact spot where Elizabeth Jennings boarded the streetcar and was assaulted, I could not find a single clue that a milestone event in the pursuit of equal rights for blacks had taken place here in this section of lower Manhattan once known as Five Points. There was no sign, plaque, or statue.

But even if you knew that something important had happened at the intersection of Pearl and Chatham streets, you'd have trouble locating the spot. That's because there is no Chatham Street anymore. It was renamed Park Row long ago. And it's not the only street in the area that has been renamed, rerouted, or changed in some way.

The only historical marker anywhere near the site in 2003 was a small green street sign that proclaimed, Joseph Doherty Corner. A young policeman standing beneath it, who told me that he was there "every day," couldn't say who Joseph Doherty is or was.

(I learned later that Doherty was a former volunteer in the Belfast Brigade of the Provisional Irish Republican Army. He escaped during a 1981 trial for murder and made his way to the United States, where he was caught and arrested in 1983. He attracted sympathizers, including celebrities and politicians. Most of the time he was in the United States he was housed at the Metropolitan Correctional Center. The street corner near his cell was renamed in an effort to call attention to his situation. After a nine-year legal battle, he was deported.)

Nearby, at Duane Street, a small alleyway had been named Cardinal Hayes Place. In Chinatown, which begins a block away to the east, Kimlau Square hosts memorials to Lin Ze Xu, a hero in China in the 1800s in part for trying to stop the opium trade, and to Benjamin Ralph Kimlau, a Chinese American who fought heroically for the United States in World War II. Kimlau Square, it turned out, was formerly known as Chatham Square.

Nothing, anywhere, about Elizabeth Jennings.

The old streetcar tracks are still there, at least partially. While most are embedded underneath layers of asphalt, some can still be seen at Kimlau Square.

A subway stop nearby strikes me in a way as a tribute to Elizabeth Jennings. Every day millions of people of many cultures, countries, and ethnicities ride shoulder-to-shoulder and think nothing of it.

Thirteen years later, in 2016, I revisited the area to see how it might have evolved. The newly built Freedom Tower, which replaced the World Trade Center, now loomed over the southern end of Manhattan. The African Burial Ground, a short walk from the site, had become a National Monument overseen by the National Park Service.

The intersection had changed little, but something caught my attention nearby. A small green street sign proclaiming Elizabeth Jennings Place had been added at the corner of Park Row and Spruce Street, which is near (but not at) the intersection where the assault occurred long ago.

Looking into this promising development, I learned that students at Public School 361, the Children's Workshop School, had worked hard to get the sign installed. With the help and guidance of the third- and fourth-grade teacher Miriam Sicherman, the students gathered signatures and petitioned the city of New York to put up the sign. They were the second group of schoolchildren to try.

In a phone interview Ms. Sicherman explained that her school undertakes a social justice project each year to coincide with the national holiday honoring the Reverend Dr. Martin Luther King, Jr. Ms. Sicherman had read a newspaper story about Elizabeth Jennings and suggested to the children that they could try to find out more about the long-forgotten schoolteacher turned activist.

"There wasn't much out there about her, but there was enough to write a play," Ms. Sicherman said. With the backing of the school's principal, Maria Velez-Clarke, Ms. Sicherman and her students set out to see if it was possible to have a playground on Pearl Street renamed in Elizabeth Jennings's honor.

They were turned down. Instead, city officials said they could have an honorary street name added for Elizabeth Jennings, although not at the intersection where Elizabeth Jennings boarded the streetcar and was assaulted. That intersection had already been renamed for someone else, Joseph Doherty.

City officials chose a nearby intersection. Ms. Sicherman and her students accepted the offer, and the sign was added in a ceremony in the spring of 2007.

Perhaps one day a plaque will explain what happened to Elizabeth Jennings. Maybe a playground will be renamed, as the students of the Children's Workshop School wished. I envision a statue in City Hall Park. There are only a handful of statues of women in New York City, and I think it's about time city leaders added another.

With its history of rebuilding and its haste to greet the future, perhaps it's not surprising that New York City sometimes forgets its past. But part of that is the fault of the people, not just New Yorkers, but all of us. Too often we think of history as a permanent series of events. The reality is that stories from the past are often forgotten. Much depends on who remembers and tells the stories from the past and how and why they are told. The contributions of black Americans, other minorities, and women have been overlooked, often deliberately. Too quickly we may conclude that if an event is not already in an official textbook, it didn't happen or it's not important. The story of Elizabeth Jennings reminds us that this is not so. Sometimes, interesting stories are right in front of us, if only we take time to look.

Chester A. Arthur being sworn in as president of the United States at his home in Manhattan.

POSTSCRIPT

Chester A. Arthur: Tragedy Leads to Presidency

THIS BOOK IS ELIZABETH JENNINGS'S STORY, but many readers may be curious about Chester A. Arthur and what happened to him after the court case.

Except for a three-month adventure to Kansas with a friend, Chester Arthur continued to live in Manhattan and work at the law firm. During the Civil War he was deeply involved with the Union cause, eventually rising to the rank of general in the Union army.

When the war was over, he became active in what was known as machine politics, the Democratic Party organization, often referred to as Tammany Hall, which played a major role in controlling New York City and New York State politics. Over time Chester Arthur became more powerful and connected. In 1880 James A. Garfield, who was running for president of the United States, chose him as his vice-presidential running mate, and they won the election.

Tragically, President Garfield, after less than four months in office, was shot by a man named Charles J. Guiteau at the Baltimore and Potomac railroad station in Washington, D.C. Garfield died eleven weeks later in Elberon, New Jersey, at the seashore where he had been taken in the hope that he might recover.

This meant that Chester Arthur became president, but it was a job he really didn't want. His wife had died the year before. He was said to never have recovered from her death. His grief, and his own failing health, affected his time in the White House.

He had other reasons to grieve as well. Like Elizabeth Jennings and her husband, Charles Graham, Chester Arthur and his wife, Ellen, lost an infant son in 1863.

While lacking the leadership skills to become an outstanding president, he had a major success by signing a series of treaties known as the Geneva Convention. The treaties dictate the humane treatment during wartime of civilians, prisoners of war (POWs), and wounded soldiers, and are still largely in effect today.

He also established what is called civil service in the federal government by signing the Pendleton Act. This meant that federal jobs were to be awarded on the basis of merit, not political connections.

When Chester Arthur became president, and again after he died in 1886, the Elizabeth Jennings story was briefly reintroduced to the public. The *New York Times*, for example, highlighted the Jennings case as one of Chester Arthur's triumphs as a young lawyer many years before.

Both Chester Arthur and Elizabeth Jennings died from complications of what was then called Bright's disease, a chronic inflammation of the kidneys. It seems likely that after that day in court in 1855, they never crossed paths again.

Near the end of President Arthur's life, on a railroad trip he took across the country, many of those waiting to greet him were black men and women. An especially supportive group honored him at the Lafayette, Indiana, train station on July 31, 1883, presenting him with a plaque thanking him for his dedication to "justice to an oppressed people." In black communities across the United States people had not forgotten that in his days as a young lawyer Chester Arthur had accepted and won an important case called *Elizabeth Jennings v. Third Avenue Railroad Company*.

A portrait of Chester A. Arthur.

Bibliography

I BEGAN RESEARCHING THE STORY of Elizabeth Jennings about twenty years ago and have consulted many libraries, archives, and historical associations. In several cases—the New York Public Library, for example—I visited multiple times to follow up one lead or another. While I was working on other book projects, sometimes the Elizabeth Jennings story had to wait, but I always returned to it when I had the chance.

Doing research takes persistence, and sometimes it can be disappointing. I have a file folder called "Dead Ends" to prove it! Below, I've listed the places where I had success with researching either online, in person, or both. If you can't visit these institutions, you can explore their websites, where you are bound to find topics that intrigue you. Who knows? You may start researching a mystery of your own.

The New York Public Library
www.nypl.org
This is one of my favorite places in the world. The librarians helped me locate obscure newspapers, kept deep in the vaults. I could not have written this book without the New York Public Library or its affiliate, the Schomburg, listed below.

The Schomburg Center for Research in Black Culture/NYPL
www.nypl.org/locations/schomburg
Located in Harlem, the Schomburg is a library designed for research. I found many little gems of information here. The staff was enormously helpful and supportive of my project.

The New-York Historical Society
www.nyhistory.org/
An amazing repository of information about New York City and State. Always a fun place to visit.

The Library of Congress
www.loc.gov/
This is the largest library in the world. I ordered rare editions of old newspapers that couldn't be located elsewhere.

Smithsonian Institution
www.si.edu
I did my research for this book before the Smithsonian's National Museum of African American History and Culture opened in September 2016, but I did find resources at other divisions of the Smithsonian, especially the National Portrait Gallery.

The National Archives and Records Administration
www.archives.gov/
A huge collection of Americana.

The United States Census of 1850 and the Census of the State of New York for 1855
www.ancestry.com/s61792/t30847/rd.ashx (for the 1850 census)
www.ancestry.com/t29419/rd.ashx (for the 1855 NYS census)
Online searches of census data helped me to locate the Jennings family, their address in Manhattan, and more. Note: Ancestry.com requires a subscription and password.

The Museum of the City of New York
www.mcny.org/
I'm always delighted by the special exhibits here. It's a short walk from a wonderful art museum, the Solomon R. Guggenheim Museum, so it's easy to visit both in one afternoon.

The New York Transit Museum
www.nytransitmuseum.org/
Want to see what an old streetcar looks like? Visit this museum in Brooklyn, New York, where one dating to 1904 is part of the collection.

Brooklyn Public Library
www.bklynlibrary.org/
Love this library! I am impressed by its book collection but also by special projects, such as digitizing old copies of the *Brooklyn Daily Eagle* newspaper, which you can access online.

The Department of Records and Information Services, City of New York, and the New York City Department of Vital Statistics
www.nyc.gov/html/records/html/home/home.shtml
I filled out an application for Elizabeth Jennings's official death certificate, providing the information I had at the time. Several weeks later a copy arrived in the mail.

Cypress Hills Cemetery, Brooklyn, New York
www.cypresshillscemetery.org/
This is where Elizabeth Jennings is buried alongside her husband, Charles Graham, and her parents, Thomas L. and Elizabeth Jennings. The grounds are open to the public, and visitors are welcome.

Rutgers, the State University of New Jersey, University Libraries
www.libraries.rutgers.edu/
With the help of several librarians, I located several hard-to-find books here.

Fairleigh Dickinson University Library
www.view2.fdu.edu/about-fdu/fdu-libraries/
The librarians here kindly loaned microfilm of several editions of old newspapers for my review.

Kansas State Historical Society
www.kshs.org/
Through e-mail correspondence with several librarians and researchers, I located a hard-to-find magazine that published two stories about Elizabeth Jennings in 1895, along with the only known photograph of her.

Ossining, New York, Historical Society
www.ossininghistorical.org/wordpress/
I visited here many times when my husband and I lived in this town, on the Hudson River north of New York City. The photo of Chester A. Arthur's "spooky" old house is in its collection.

Books include:

Anbinder, Tyler. *Five Points: The 19th Century New York City Neighborhood that Invented Tap Dance, Stole Elections, and Became the World's Most Notorious Slum.* **New York: Plume, 2002.**
A detailed study of the Five Points neighborhood, this book was chosen as one of the New York Public Library's "25 Books to Remember."

Beatty, Barbara. *Preschool Education in America: The Culture of Young Children from the Colonial Era to the Present.* **New Haven: Yale University Press, 1995.**
An academic book that was an important resource for me.

Brinkley, Alan. *The Unfinished Nation: A Concise History of the American People.* **New York: McGraw-Hill Higher Education, 1993.**
An overview of American history that is a great resource for teachers.

Burrows, Edwin G., and Mike Wallace. *Gotham: A History of New York City to 1898.* **New York: Oxford University Press, 1999.**
A Pulitzer Prize–winning book about New York City's early years. Fun to browse.

Dickens, Charles. *American Notes for Circulation in Two Volumes*, vol. 1. **London: Chapman and Hall, 1842.**
The famous English novelist offended many Americans when he published his accounts, often unflattering, of his travels in the United States.

Duffy, John. *A History of Public Health in New York City 1625–1866.* **New York: Russell Sage Foundation, 1968.**
A fact-filled book that provided a treasure chest of facts.

Ernst, Robert. *Immigrant Life in New York City 1825–1863.* **Syracuse, New York: Syracuse University Press, 1994.**
An academic book that provided insight on the experiences of immigrants in New York City.

Foner, Eric. *Gateway to Freedom: The Hidden History of the Underground Railroad.* **New York: W. W. Norton, 2015.**
One of my favorite author-historians. This book, like others written by him, is a fascinating read.

Gellman, David N., and David Quigley, eds. *Jim Crow New York: A Documentary History of Race and Citizenship 1777–1877.* **New York: New York University Press, 2003.**
An academic book that was a helpful resource for me.

Harris, Leslie M. *In the Shadow of Slavery: African Americans in New York City 1626–1863.* **Chicago: University of Chicago Press, 2003.**
A carefully researched, scholarly book.

Hearth, Amy Hill. *"Strong Medicine" Speaks: A Native American Elder Has Her Say: An Oral History.* **New York: Atria Books/Simon & Schuster, 2008.**
I wrote this book about the mother of the chief of the Nanticoke Lenni-Lenape Tribal Nation. They are related to the original people who lived on Manhattan Island for thousands of years.

Homberger, Eric, and Alice Hudson, cartographic consultant. *The Historical Atlas of New York City: A Visual Celebration of Nearly 400 Years of New York City's History.* **New York: Henry Holt, 1994.**
If you love maps, you'll enjoy this book. Studying it provides a good way to understand the growth of and changes in Manhattan.

Hood, Clifton. *722 Miles: The Building of the Subways and How They Transformed New York.* **Baltimore: Johns Hopkins University Press, 1993.**
The building of the NYC subway system is an incredible feat. This academic book explains how it was done.

Hoose, Phillip. *Claudette Colvin: Twice Toward Justice.* **New York: Melanie Kroupa Books/Farrar Straus Giroux, 2009.**
I was so inspired by this book, which tells the story of a teenager who took a stand on a segregated bus in Montgomery, Alabama, almost a year prior to Rosa Parks. A winner of the National Book Award for Young People's Literature, this book is perfect for middle school readers and up.

Howe, George Frederick. *Chester A. Arthur: A Quarter-Century of Machine Politics.* **New York: Frederick Ungar Publishing, 1935; republished 1957.**
There aren't many books on Arthur, so this biography was invaluable to me.

Kelley, Blair L. M. *Right to Ride: Streetcar Boycotts and African American Citizenship in the Era of Plessy v. Ferguson.* **Chapel Hill: University of North Carolina Press, 2010.**
Dr. Kelley's focus is on the struggles to fight segregation in New Orleans, La., Richmond, Virginia, and Savannah, Georgia. A fascinating scholarly book.

Kliebard, Herbert M. *The Struggle for the American Curriculum,* **2d ed. New York: Routledge, 1994.**
Purely academic and written for education professionals.

Koeppel, Gerard. *Water for Gotham: A History.* **Princeton, N.J.: Princeton University Press, 2000.**
You wouldn't think an academic book about drinking water could be this fascinating, but it is. At the same time it offers terrific insight into the growth and challenges of early New York.

McCabe, James D. *The Life of Gen. Chester A. Arthur, addendum to From the Farm to the Presidential Chair: The Life and Public Services of Gen. James A. Garfield.* Philadelphia: National Publishing, 1880.
Biography of President Garfield, with an added section about Chester A. Arthur. This book was intended for historians and presidential scholars.

Meinig, D. W. *The Shaping of America: A Geographical Perspective on 500 Years of History, vol. 2, Continental America, 1800–1867.* New Haven and London: Yale University Press, 1993.
One of five volumes of interest to college-level students and researchers in the field of geography.

Merwick, Donna. *The Shame and the Sorrow: The Dutch-Amerindian Encounters in New Netherland.* Philadelphia: University of Pennsylvania Press, 2006.
Most people know very little about the Native people of New York and New Jersey. This book tells part of their tragic story.

Ovington, Mary White. *Half a Man: The Status of the Negro in New York.* London: Longmans, Green, 1911; reprinted New York: Negro Universities Press, 1969.
A groundbreaking book by a woman author. The book includes a brief account of Elizabeth Jennings's story.

Reeves, Thomas C. *Gentleman Boss: The Life and Times of Chester Alan Arthur.* Newtown, Conn.: American Political Biography Press, 1975.
Like the book by George Frederick Howe listed earlier, this book is a rare look at the life of Arthur. I'm grateful that it was written.

Rury, John L. *Education and Social Change: Contours in the History of American Schooling*, 5th ed. New York: Routledge, 2016.
An academic book included in the curricula of many graduate schools of education in the United States.

Schlesinger, Arthur M., Jr., gen. ed., and John S. Bowman, exec. ed. *The Almanac of American History.* New York: Barnes & Noble, by arrangement with the Putnam Grosset Group, 1993.
This book provides a year-by-year synopsis of historical events in America. A great resource for teachers.

Shi, David E., and George Brown Tindall. *America, a Narrative History.*, 5th ed. New York: W. W. Norton. 1999.
A college-level textbook assigned to students in many high school advanced placement U.S. history classes.

Stansell, Christine. *City of Women: Sex and Class in New York, 1789–1860.* Urbana and Chicago: University of Illinois Press, 1987.
Academic book about women in New York City during the time Elizabeth Jennings lived.

Thornton, J. Mills, III. *Dividing Lines: Municipal Politics and the Struggle for Civil Rights in Montgomery, Birmingham, and Selma.* Tuscaloosa: University of Alabama Press, 2002.
An extremely thorough, scholarly account of the modern civil rights movement in three southern cities.

Tocqueville de, Alexis. *Democracy in America*; **first printing 1835.**
A fascinating lens on the United States in its early days.

Tomes, Nancy: *The Gospel of Germs: Men, Women, and the Microbe in American Life.*
Cambridge, Mass.: Harvard University Press, 1998.
A creepy but unforgettable academic-level book.

White, Shane: *Stories of Freedom in Black New York.* **Cambridge, Mass.: Harvard University Press, 2002.**
Valuable information about segregation in NYC, including the city's theatrical culture.

Newspapers: An Invaluable and Fascinating Source

The Liberator (antislavery newspaper published in Boston by a white man named William Lloyd Garrison)

The Colored American (black-owned newspaper published in New York)

New-York Daily Tribune (general-interest newspaper published by Horace Greeley, a white man who was progressive about equal rights for blacks)

The North Star (Frederick Douglass's first newspaper)

Frederick Douglass' Paper (*The North Star* renamed)

Douglass' Monthly (a supplement to *Frederick Douglass' Paper*, and then an independent paper)

National Anti-Slavery Standard (weekly newspaper of the American Anti-Slavery Society)

The Anglo-African Magazine (black-owned newspaper published in New York)

New York Age (black-owned newspaper)

New York Times (general-interest newspaper still published)

Brooklyn Daily Eagle (general-interest newspaper published in Brooklyn, N.Y.)

New York World (general-interest newspaper published in New York)

(New Orleans) Picayune (general-interest newspaper still published)

The Pacific Appeal (black-owned newspaper published in San Francisco)

Municipal Reports

The Brooklyn City and Kings County Record: A Budget of General Information

Annual Report of the City Inspector of the City of New York

Journals and Magazines

John H. Hewitt, "The Search for Elizabeth Jennings, Heroine of a Sunday Afternoon in New York City," *New York History: the Quarterly Journal of the New York State Historical Society* (October 1990).

Leo H. Hirsch, Jr., "The Free Negro in New York," *Journal of Negro History*, vol. 16, issue 4 (October 1931).

Daniel Perlman, "Organizations of the Free Negro in New York City, 1800–1860," *Journal of Negro History*, vol. 56, issue 3, (July 1971).

H. Cordelia Ray, "The Story of an Old Wrong," *The American Woman's Journal* (July 1895).

H. Cordelia Ray, "The First Free Kindergarten for Colored Children," ibid.

Websites

New York City Department of Parks and Recreation regarding Mannahatta Park: www.nycgovparks.org/parks/manahatta-park/highlights/19696
This is a small park near what was once the New York Municipal Slave Market.

National Humanities Center, TeacherServe (registered trademark) on segregation: www.nationalhumanitiescenter.org/tserve/freedom/1865-1917/essays/segregation.htm

Teachers will want to take a look at "Freedom's Story: Segregation" on p. 1 by Steven F. Lawson, National Humanities Center fellow, Department of History, Rutgers, State University of New Jersey.

The main web address TeacherServe (registered trademark), a curriculum research service from the National Humanities Center, is www.nationalhumanitiescenter.org/tserve/tsaboutus.htm

For information about the African Burial Ground National Monument, see website of the National Park Service at www.nps.gov/afbg/index.htm.
If you visit Manhattan, be sure to plan on spending time here.

The New-York Historical Society's website, which provides information about African Free Schools. The link is www.nyhistory.org/web/africanfreeschool/history/context.html.

The Division of Rare and Manuscript Collections at Cornell University, at www.rare.library.cornell.edu/, provided details about William Lloyd Garrison. The same was true of Lehigh University's "The Vault at Pfaff's: An Archive of Art and Literature by the Bohemians of Antebellum New York," at www.pfaffs.web.lehigh.edu/, which I accessed for information on Horace Greeley.

For a source on Joseph Doherty, I came across a March 13, 2015, article titled "Joe Doherty Corner: The Troubles in America," by Rachel Aileen Searcy, published in *Archives of Irish America, The Back Table: Archives and Special Collections at New York University*. The direct link is www.wp.nyu.edu/specialcollections/2015/03/13/joe-doherty-corner-the-troubles-in-america/.

Notes

THE NOTES LISTED HERE refer to sources of material. References are to books and articles mentioned in the Bibliography.

Part I: A Day like No Other

"Three Notes About Language": The *Colored American* was a black-owned newspaper: sources include *Gateway to Freedom,* 7. "Colored" churches, *Gotham,* 855, 548.

The term *civil rights* has been replaced with *equal rights for blacks* to avoid confusion; *civil rights* is a term used mainly in regard to the 1950s, not 1850s. Source: Dr. Amy Bass, professor of history, College of New Rochelle, New Rochelle, New York.

1. "Those Monsters in Human Form"

As an unmarried lady in her twenties: The year of Elizabeth's birth is sometimes said to be 1827 and at other times, 1830. Birth records were not kept in the careful way they are today.

"There was no Brooklyn Bridge or Statue of Liberty": The Brooklyn Bridge was completed in 1883. The Statue of Liberty was opened to the public in 1886. Long Acre Square was renamed Times Square in 1904: *The Historical Atlas of New York City,* 175. Development of Rockefeller Center began in 1930. The Empire State Building was opened to the public in 1931: from *Gotham* and *The Historical Atlas of New York City.*

Garbage in the streets: *Five Points,* 82–83.

Sewers: ibid., 85–86.

"The city of New York was made up of Manhattan": *Gotham,* 660–62.

Drought in 1854: *Brooklyn Daily Eagle* and other sources.

Diseases in New York City: *Immigrant Life in New York City 1825–1863,* 22.

Five Points was named for the "five-cornered intersection of Anthony, Orange, and Cross Streets": from *Five Points,* 14, whose author, Tyler Anbinder, notes that "defining the borders of a neighborhood is not easy." He adds that *Frank Leslie's Illustrated Newspaper* in 1873 defined Five Points as "bounded by Canal Street, the Bowery, Chatham, Pearl and Centre

Streets, forming a truncated triangle about one mile square," footnote, 17. The boundaries of the neighborhood are different in *Gangs of New York*, which describes it as "roughly, the territory bounded by Broadway, Canal Street, the Bowery and Park Row, formerly Chatham Street," in colonial times (1) and "the intersection of Baxter, Worth and Park Streets" (5) in 1927, when the book was first published.

Charles Dickens on the conditions of Five Points: from his *American Notes for Circulation in Two Volumes*, vol. 1, 99.

The Jennings family home was located at 167 Church Street in the Fifth Ward of Manhattan: 1850 U.S. Census.

Sarah E. Adams: from Elizabeth Jennings's firsthand account published by the *New-York Daily Tribune*, July 19, 1854.

Sidebar "The First New Yorkers: Manhattan" called "the island of the hills": *The Shame and the Sorrow*, 10. Information about the Lenni-Lenape people from *"Strong Medicine" Speaks: A Native American Elder Has Her Say*, 6. The Dutch arrived in 1614: *Gotham*, 19; the English arrived in 1664: ibid., 75.

2: Stray Dogs and Pickpockets

Description and details about horse-drawn trolleys and omnibuses: New York Transit Museum website and *722 Miles: The Building of the Subways and How They Transformed New York*.

"In the twenty years since the first horse railway was launched": The world's first horse railway (or horse-drawn streetcar) was launched by the New York and Harlem Railroad in 1832: ibid., 37. By 1860 there were fourteen horse railroad companies in Manhattan: ibid., 40.

Businesses in Five Points included printshops and manufacturers of shoes and tobacco products: *Gotham*, 475.

Children as pickpockets: *Five Points*, 220.

Black peddlers sold buttermilk and straw for bedding: *Five Points*, 119.

"Hot corn all hot": *City of Women*, 14.

Hot corn was not popcorn, but "freshly cooked ears of sweet corn" in season: *Five Points*, 129.

Sources for information on Horatio Alger, Jr., include *Gotham*, 977–78.

Sidebar "Slavery in the North":

"New York City even had its own slave market, located where Wall Street met the East River": *The Historical Atlas of New York City*, 44.

New York's Municipal Slave Market, at Mannahatta Park: details from the website of the New York City Department of Parks and Recreation, address listed in Bibliography.

The African Burial Ground National Monument: website of the National Park Service, address listed in Bibliography.

Sidebar "Timeline, the End of Slavery in Northern States": *Jim Crow New York*, 19–23, and the following sources for the end of slavery by state:

MASSACHUSETTS: www.mass.gov/courts/court-info/sjc/edu-res-center/abolition/abolition1-gen.html

PENNSYLVANIA: www.phmc.state.pa.us/portal/communities/documents/1776-1865/abolition-slavery.html

RHODE ISLAND: www.ir.uiowa.edu/cgi/viewcontent.cgi?article=4956&context=etd

CONNECTICUT: www.connecticuthistory.org/topics-page/slavery-and-abolition/

NEW YORK: www.nyhistory.org/community/slavery-end-new-york-state

NEW JERSEY: www.academic.udayton.edu/race/02rights/slave08.htm

OHIO, INDIANA, ILLINOIS, MICHIGAN, IOWA, WISCONSIN, and MINNESOTA, MAINE, NEW HAMPSHIRE, KANSAS, and VERMONT: www.mtholyoke.edu/~kmporter/slaverytimeline.htm

CALIFORNIA: www.sfmuseum.org/hist5/caladmit.html

OREGON: www.ohs.org/research-and-library/oregon-historical-quarterly/upload/02_Smith_
Oregon-s-Civil-War_115_2_Summer-2014.pdf
NEVADA: www.onlinenevada.org/articles/nevada-statehood
WEST VIRGINIA: www.wvculture.org/history///africanamericans/slaveryabolished01.html

3. A City Divided by Race

Voting restrictions by race in New York: *Gotham*, 512–14.
Free blacks in the North were denied the right to vote except in Maine, Vermont, New
Hampshire, and Massachusetts, according to *American Slavery*, 82. "Winning the Vote: A
History of Voting Rights," by Steven Mintz, Gilder Lehrman Institute of American History,
however, includes Rhode Island in that list: www.gilderlehrman.org/history-by-era/government-
and-civics/essays/winning-vote-history-voting-rights. Both sources state that in New York black
residents could vote but only if they met a property requirement. Also regarding voting in New
York, see www.nycourts.gov/history/legal-history-new-york/documents/Publications_1821-NY-
Constitution.pdf.

Voting rights for women: *The Unfinished Nation*, 640.
Segregated schools: *Journal of Negro History*, vol. 16, issue 4, 426–33 (Oct. 1931).
Schools for black children in New York City described as "dark, damp, small, and cheerless":
New-York Daily Tribune, March 8, 1859.
Jobs available to black New Yorkers: multiple sources, including *Journal of Negro History*,
vol. 16, issue 4, 438 (Oct. 1931) and *Jim Crow New York*, 17. Black men as chimney sweeps:
Five Points, 91.
In 1855 there were 13 black teachers in New York City, out of a total of 1,356: *Immigrant
Life in New York City 1825–1863*, 217.
"What are my prospects?": *Gotham*, 547.
Segregation in churches: *Gateway to Freedom*, 59.
Segregation by neighborhood: *In the Shadow of Slavery: African Americans in New York
City 1626–1863*, 266–67; also, *Five Points*, 97.
Theaters, "among the first institutions to be segregated in New York": *Stories of Freedom in
Black New York*, 80.
Segregated hotels and restaurants in New York City: "Freedom's Story: Segregation," website,
National Humanities Center, address listed in Bibliography.
Rules on streetcars that forced blacks to ride on the outside of New York City streetcars or
to wait for one carrying a sign that stated COLORED PEOPLE ALLOWED IN THE CAR:
Gotham, 856; also, *New York Times*, Jan. 1, 1880.
"Colored" streetcars in New York City were often called Jim Crow cars after a minstrel
character of that name became an insulting term used by whites to describe black people:
Gotham, 856.
Information about the origins of the term *Jim Crow* for sidebar "What Was Jim Crow?": *Jim
Crow New York*, 3–4, and *Gotham*, 856.

4. "I Screamed Murder with All My Voice" and 5. "You Will Sweat for This!'"

Source for both chapters: Elizabeth Jennings herself in her account published by the
New-York Daily Tribune, July 19, 1854.

6: An Admired Family

Thomas Jennings marched with others as a young man through the streets of lower
Manhattan: *Anglo-African Magazine*, April 1859.
Many sources refer to Elizabeth's father as an activist. Thomas Jennings "worked in the African

Society for Mutual Relief and helped found the Abyssinian Baptist Church": *Gotham*, 856.

The most complete source on the life of Thomas Jennings comes from an obituary or tribute written by Frederick Douglass, published in *Douglass' Monthly*, March 1859 and reprinted in *The Anglo-African Magazine*, April 1859, includes details about Elizabeth and her siblings.

Thomas Jennings's shop at Nassau and Chatham streets: *Douglass' Monthly*, March 1859.

Thomas Jennings, inventor: ibid. Patent signed by John Quincy Adams: *Douglass' Monthly*, March 1859.

Elizabeth's mother, a daughter of Jacob Cartwright, a black soldier in the Revolutionary War: *Frederick Douglass' Paper*, March 2, 1855.

African Free Schools, New-York Historical Society's website, address listed in Bibliography. The names of the Jennings children—William, Thomas, Jr., Matilda, and Elizabeth—are mentioned in various publications, such as *The Colored American, Douglass' Monthly*, and the *New-York Daily Tribune*. Matilda shows up in the U.S. Census, on a Freedman's Bank record, and on the tombstone in the Jennings family plot in Brooklyn, N.Y. Another sister, Lucy, is mentioned by Frederick Douglass (*Douglass' Monthly*, March 1859). She evidently married and moved to San Francisco (*Pacific Appeal*, May 16, 1863). Elizabeth herself refers to at least four brothers and sisters in a letter to the editor published by *New York Age*, Sept. 20, 1890.

In this letter, she wrote of their very unusual educational opportunities: "Another school was opened . . . and four of my brothers and sisters were the first pupils enrolled. This was the nucleus of colored teachers in the city of New York."

The Ladies' Literary Society, coverage of essay, and essay itself, recited by Elizabeth Jennings: *The Colored American*, Sept. 23, 1837.

Recitations by children as teaching method and as a form of popular entertainment: *The Struggle for the American Curriculum*, 479.

Sidebar "Who Should Go to School?":

Education for girls unequal to that for boys and meant to make them be better mothers and wives: *Education and Social Change*, 89–90.

Climbing stairs too often might be a danger to their health: ibid., 94.

Sidebar "Frederick Douglass and the Black Press": *The Almanac of American History*, 267, and *The Unfinished Nation*, 358. Regarding Frederick Douglass's publications: www.loc.gov/collections/frederick-douglass-papers/articles-and-essays/frederick-douglass-timeline/1847-to-1859/

Black newspapers: "The Free Negro in New York," *Journal of Negro History*, 444-46. While Hirsch, the author, credits John B. Russwurm as the founder of *Freedom's Journal*, the authors of *Gotham* assert that it was Russwurm along with Rev. Samuel Cornish, William Hamilton, and Rev. Peter Williams, Jr., 549. Information on *The Colored American* from *Gotham*, p. 855.

Frederick Douglass referred to Elizabeth's conduct as "courageous" and "beyond all praise": *Frederick Douglass' Paper*, March 2, 1855.

7: A "Shameful" and "Loathsome" Issue

"An emergency meeting was held at the church": from Elizabeth Jennings's published account.

Letter by David L. Child, Anti-Slavery Society, describing segregated conditions in the North: *The Liberator* May 7, 1831.

Letter by Frederick Douglass describing "the brutal manner in which colored persons are uniformly treated in steamers on the Hudson River": *The Liberator*, June 11, 1847.

Writer reports incident on uptown streetcar: *New-York Daily Tribune*, September 7, 1850.

Conductors, not passengers, to blame: letter to the editor, *New-York Daily Tribune*, September 16, 1850.

Sidebar "Trying to Make a Difference" *The Liberator*, June 14, 1834.

Sidebar "William Lloyd Garrison": The *Unfinished Nation*, 357, and *America, a Narrative History*, 633–34, and the Division of Rare and Manuscript Collections, Cornell University: www.rare.library.cornell.edu/.

Sidebar "Horace Greeley": *The Almanac of American History*, p. 323; *The Unfinished Nation*, p. 462; and *America, a Narrative History*, 537, 649; *Gotham*, 525; Lehigh University: The Vault at Pfaff's: An Archive of Art and Literature by the Bohemians of Antebellum New York. www.pfaffs.web.lehigh.edu/

8. A Future U.S. President

Erastus Culver: *Gentleman Boss*, 14.

Family background of Chester A. Arthur: sources include *Gentleman Boss* and *The Life of Gen. Chester A. Arthur.*

Chester Arthur made a good impression on Erastus Culver; law firm name changed to Culver, Parker, and Arthur: *Gentleman Boss*, 14. Also, *New York World*, "Preparing for the Burial," November 20, 1886.

Address of law firm Culver & Parker: *Chester A. Arthur, a Quarter-Century of Machine Politics*, 12.

Sidebar "Chester Arthur: His Early Years":

Chester's college pranks: *Gentleman Boss*, 8–9.

Essay by Chester Arthur in which he argued that slavery infected the very soul of the nation itself: Arthur Papers, New-York Historical Society, 1847.

Sidebar "The Fugitive Slave Act": *Gateway to Freedom*, 124–25, 134, 136.

The number of black residents in New York City decreased from 16,358 in 1840 to 13,815 in 1850; from 1850 to 1855, declined to 11,740: *In the Shadow of Slavery*, 274–75.

The total population of the city had surged in 1855 to a new high of nearly 630,000 because of white immigration: *Immigrant Life in New York City 1825–1863*, 20.

9: Elizabeth Jennings v. Third Avenue Railroad Company

Lawsuit filed in Brooklyn: *Brooklyn Daily Eagle*, Feb. 23, 1855.

The conductor and the driver chose not to fight the lawsuit: ibid.

"What they really wanted was to change the system": letter by Thomas L. Jennings to Elizabeth's supporters, published in *The American Woman's Journal.*

Among the judges was a man named William Rockwell: *The Brooklyn City and Kings County Record: A Budget of General Information.*

The courtroom was "crowded almost to suffocation"; the black community hoped that it would be a test case: *New York Times*, in a story about Chester A. Arthur, Jan. 1, 1880.

We do not know the exact list of witnesses who testified or if black witnesses, including Elizabeth Jennings, were permitted to testify. It is possible that Chester Arthur, acting as Elizabeth's attorney, read aloud her letter describing the events on the streetcar. The original transcripts consisting of handwritten notes are said to have been lost in a historic 1911 fire that destroyed the New York State Library in Albany, New York.

Elizabeth was allowed to be a plaintiff; this was not unusual by this time in New York: "The presence of blacks in court on their own behalf became familiar [in New York] by the late 1820s," according to *In the Shadow of Slavery*, 105.

Judge Rockwell's instructions to the jury: *Brooklyn Daily Eagle*, Feb. 23, 1855.

Sidebar "Getting to Brooklyn": East River frozen: *Annual Report of the City Inspector of the City of New York for the Year* includes a chart showing that the month of February 1855 was much colder than usual.

Painting, crossing from Brooklyn to Manhattan on the ice, 1852: Brooklyn Public Library.

10: The Jury's Decision

"A Wholesome Verdict": *New-York Daily Tribune*, Feb. 23, 1855.

"Rights of Coloured People Vindicated": *National Anti-Slavery Standard*, March 3, 1855.

"Legal Rights Vindicated": *Frederick Douglass' Paper*, March 2, 1855.

The Third Avenue Railroad Company, followed shortly by the other streetcar companies, moved quickly to integrate their cars: *Gentleman Boss*, 16, states that "all New York city railroad companies integrated their cars." Other sources state that three of the four operating in Manhattan did.

"Railroads, steamboats, omnibuses, and ferry boats will be admonished [warned] from this, as to the rights of respectable colored people": *New-York Daily Tribune*, Feb. 23, 1855.

Success of *Elizabeth Jennings v. Third Avenue Railroad Company* considered "the first major breakthrough" in ending discriminatory practices in public transportation in NYC: *Gotham*, 856.

Setbacks: *Gotham*, 857.

Success of court case led to founding of the Legal Rights' Association in New York City; one of the founders was Thomas Jennings: *Douglass' Monthly*, March 1859.

February 22, the date of Elizabeth's court victory, was celebrated for years in New York: *Gentleman Boss*, 16.

Part II: A Forgotten Hero

11: An Uncanny Similarity to Rosa Parks

Details about the arrest of Rosa Parks: From *Dividing Lines*, p. 45–61.

Advertisements in a southern newspaper: *New-Orleans Picayune*, July 18, 1854.

Nearly four million black men, women, and children were enslaved in the South at the start of the Civil War in 1860: *American Slavery*, 93.

Free black people estimated at about 226,000 in 1860 in the North and about 260,000 in the South: ibid., 253.

She refers to herself as Elizabeth Jennings Graham: letter to the editor, *New York Age*, Sept. 20, 1890.

12: What Happened to Elizabeth Jennings?

Details of the Civil War: *The Shaping of America*, 528.

Death of Thomas Jennings: *Douglass' Monthly*, March 1859. Died Feb. 11, 1859, at age sixty-eight (born 1791).

On June 18, 1860, Elizabeth "Jinnings" (sic) married Charles Graham: *Anglo-African Magazine*, June 30, 1860.

Elizabeth and her husband had one child, a boy named Thomas, who died at age one: *Half a Man*, 25.

Elizabeth, her husband, and her mother left New York for Monmouth County, New Jersey: 1870 U.S. Census shows Elizabeth, her sister Matilda, and their mother living in Ocean, Monmouth County, N.J.

Charles Graham, Elizabeth's husband, died in Long Branch, N.J., in 1867: records filled out by Elizabeth at Freedman's Bank in Manhattan in 1871.

Elizabeth, her sister Matilda, and their mother continued to live at the New Jersey seashore in or near a place called Eatontown for several more years: 1870 U.S. Census.

In 1871, after eight years in New Jersey, Elizabeth and her mother moved back to Manhattan, residing at 543 Broome St. Elizabeth began working as a teacher at the 41st Street School: National Archives and Records Administration, Freedman's Bank records, 1865–1871. Elizabeth made a bank deposit of $240 on Sept. 28, 1871.

According to Hewitt's article for *New York History* (October 1990), earlier in her career Elizabeth taught at Colored Public School No. 2, about 1848–1849; Promotion Society School No. 2 (part of the New York Society for the Promotion of Education Among Colored Children), 19 Thomas St., 1849–1850; Promotion Society School No. 1, 1850–1851, held at St. Philip's Church; transferred back to Promotion Society School No. 2, 1851–1853; Boys' Department of the Board of Education's Colored School No. 5, 19 Thomas St., 1854–1857, and 101 Hudson St. 1858–1862. In 1858 or 1859, she studied for and earned a Certificate of Qualification, a credential newly required by the city.

Death of Elizabeth's mother, 1873: tombstone, Cypress Hills Cemetery, Brooklyn, N.Y.

Elizabeth appears to have outlived all her siblings. Her brother William died in 1840: *The Colored American*, Oct. 24, 1840. Thomas, Jr., who had studied dentistry in Boston and set up a private practice in New Orleans, died there Jan. 31, 1862: *The Pacific Appeal*, Sept. 27, 1862. Matilda seems to have died in 1886: tombstone, Cypress Hills Cemetery, Brooklyn, N.Y. And there is no further mention, after 1863, of Lucy.

With two other black women, founded the first free kindergarten for black children in NYC; the school was held at her home; details about the school: *The American Woman's Journal*, July 1895.

Died at home, 237 W. 41st St., Manhattan, June 5, 1901: Hewitt, *New York History*.

Burial at Cypress Hills Cemetery, Brooklyn, N.Y., in Jennings family plot: confirmed by author with cemetery administrators, 2016.

Sidebar, "The Civil War Draft Riots": *Gotham*, 888–91; *In the Shadow of Slavery*, 279–86; *Five Points*, 315. In response to the riots, the federal government did back down, reducing the number of men who were selected for the draft: *Gotham*, 895–99.

Sidebar, "The First Free Kindergarten for Colored Children in NYC": Kindergarten as a new concept and philosophy: *Preschool Education in America*, 38–42; kindergarten invented by Froebel in Germany in 1837: 40; New York and Boston took the lead on starting kindergartens that were free: 73.

13: How a Creepy Old House Led to the Writing of this Book
House on Havell Street in Ossining, New York, was residence of Chester A. Arthur: Ossining Historical Society.

14: Retracing Her Footsteps
Park Row was formerly called Chatham Street: *Gangs of New York*, 1.

Interview by author of Miriam Sicherman, Nov. 19, 2016.

Joseph Doherty: "Joe Doherty Corner: The Troubles in America" by Rachel Aileen Searcy, *Archives of Irish America, The Back Table: Archives and Special Collections at New York University*, March 13, 2015, https://wp.nyu.edu/specialcollections/2015/03/13/joe-doherty-corner-the-troubles-in-america/.

Postscript: Chester A. Arthur: Tragedy Leads to Presidency

Chester Arthur's life as a Union army general, politician, vice president, and president of the United States: *Gentleman Boss* and *The Life of Gen. Chester A. Arthur*.

Chester Arthur and his wife, Ellen, lost an infant son in 1863: "News of Chester Arthur's Death: The Last Resting Place," *New York Times*, Nov. 19, 1886.

His interest in equality was never forgotten by black Americans, and in Lafayette, Ind., black leaders presented him with a plaque thanking him for his dedication to "justice to an oppressed people": *Gentleman Boss*, 365.

Author's Note about Elizabeth Jennings's Age in 1854

In some accounts, and especially on the internet, Elizabeth Jennings is sometimes said to have been twenty-four years old when she was assaulted on the streetcar in Manhattan.

I am inclined to believe she was twenty-seven.

Why is her date of birth so unclear?

Records of births were not documented in the United States in the meticulous way they are today. Babies were born at home. Sometimes midwives or doctors kept records of their own, but often the only record of a child's birth might be written by a relative in a family Bible.

Census reports done periodically by the government are crucial sources for journalists and historians, and for the most part they are reliable. However, much depended on the thoroughness (and the handwriting!) of each person hired to ask questions and fill out census forms in a designated area.

The U.S. Census of 1850, for example, states that Elizabeth Jennings was twenty years old that year (therefore, twenty-four when she was assaulted). Yet the New York State Census of 1855 also states that she was twenty. Therefore, it doesn't seem wise, in this instance, to rely on the U.S. Census.

Thomas Jennings's age is reported variously as well. The U.S. Census of 1850 states that he was "50," or born in about 1800. But a more reliable source in this particular case is a tribute to, or obituary of, him. It was written by Frederick Douglass, who reported that Thomas died Feb. 11, 1859, at sixty-eight. That would mean the year of Thomas's birth was 1791, which matches the date on his tombstone at Cypress Hills Cemetery in Brooklyn, New York.

Meanwhile, on a bank record from Sept. 28, 1871, Elizabeth Jennings's age was reported as "40." If she had indeed been forty in 1871, she would have been born in 1830 or 1831 depending on her birthday. This would mean she was about twenty-four at the time of the assault. However, a close look at the bank record indicates that the form was filled out by a clerk, not by Elizabeth. That makes it much less reliable. A bank clerk at that time would not have asked a woman her age. He would have guessed.

Cypress Hills Cemetery, where Elizabeth is buried, lists her birth date as 1830 on its website. However, a clerk contacted by e-mail said there were no cemetery records that could confirm that date. The gravestone meanwhile favors the theory that Elizabeth Jennings was twenty-seven at the time of the assault because it reads, "Died June 5, 1901, age 74 years." It does not state a date of birth.

A death certificate acquired from New York City matches the gravestone, stating that she was seventy-four when she died in 1901. This, too, indicates that she was born in 1827 and was therefore twenty-seven, not twenty-four, when she was assaulted on the streetcar in 1854.

Suggested Reading

I Am Rosa Parks, by Rosa Parks and Jim Haskins. Illustrations by Wil Clay. New York: Penguin Young Readers, 1999.

Rosa Parks: My Story, by Rosa Parks and Jim Haskins. New York: Puffin Books, reprint ed., 1999.

Claudette Colvin: Twice Toward Justice, by Phillip Hoose. New York: Melanie Kroupa Books/Farrar Straus Giroux, 2009.

Maritcha: a 19th Century American Girl, by Tonya Bolden. New York: Harry N. Abrams, 2015.

Elizabeth Jennings's Life within a Historical Timeline

1827: Elizabeth Jennings is born in New York. This is also the year slavery finally ended for all enslaved persons in New York State.

1840 to 1861: Harriet Tubman leads to freedom at least three hundred enslaved people, including her parents.

1850: Fugitive Slave Act passed.

July 16, 1854: Elizabeth Jennings is assaulted on a streetcar by a white conductor, driver, and policeman in New York City.

February 22, 1855: Elizabeth Jennings's case heard in court. Judge William Rockwell states that public transportation in New York City should not be segregated.

1857: Dred Scott decision, in which the U.S. Supreme Court affirms the right of slave owners to take their slaves into western territories. Decision is notable, also, for the fact that the "plaintiff," a man named Dred Scott, was said to not be a citizen and was therefore without standing to file the suit.

April 12, 1861: Civil War begins.

January 1, 1863: President Lincoln signs Emancipation Proclamation.

July 13 through July 16, 1863: Civil War draft riots in New York. Elizabeth Jennings, her husband, Charles Graham, and her mother leave the city for the safety of the New Jersey seashore.

May 9, 1865: Civil War ends.

December 18, 1865: Thirteenth Amendment to the Constitution is ratified. Slavery is abolished in the United States.

Civil Rights Act of 1866: This law defines all persons born in the United States (except American Indians) as citizens with equal rights.

July 28, 1868: Fourteenth Amendment to the Constitution entered into force, overturning the Dred Scott decision and granting citizenship and equal, civil, and legal rights to blacks.

March 30, 1870: Fifteenth Amendment formally adopted, granting black men the right to vote.

1865–1877: Reconstruction Era, in which former Confederate states were drawn back into the Union.

1890s: The Jim Crow era in the South—legalized discrimination against black people—begins. (Laws stay on the books until the1960s.)

April 1895: Elizabeth Jennings, with two other black women, founds the first free kindergarten for black children in New York City. The school is established in her home at 237 West Forty-first Street.

May 18, 1896: *Plessy v. Ferguson* case decided. Supreme Court upholds a Louisiana statute requiring railroads to segregate rail cars by providing "equal but separate accommodations for the white and colored races."

June 5, 1901: Elizabeth Jennings dies in New York City.

Important Locations

- The church where Elizabeth Jennings was organist, and where she was heading the day of the assault, was the First Colored American Congregational Church, on Sixth Street near the Bowery. The church was torn down long ago.

- The Jennings family home was at 167 Church Street in Manhattan. Today it is a six-story apartment building with a flower shop and café on the ground floor.

- The sign that reads ELIZABETH JENNINGS PLACE is at the corner of Spruce Street and Park Row. The actual location of the streetcar stop where the assault on Elizabeth Jennings began is at Pearl Street and Park Row. (Park Row was previously called Chatham Street.)

- The corner where the streetcar stopped, a policeman came on board, and Elizabeth was ejected from the car was at the corner of Walker Street and the Bowery. Today this intersection is known as Bowery and Canal.

- The New York Municipal Slave Market was located where Wall Street met the East River.

- The old building of Harper & Brothers (publisher of this book) was at 331 Pearl Street.

- The African Burial Ground National Monument is at 290 Broadway between Duane and Reade streets.

Acknowledgments

Sometimes a writer comes across a story that simply must be told, and no format other than a book published by a first-rate publisher can do it justice. The fact is, however, that no one creates such a book on his or her own. The writer needs a team of talented professionals. And it helps to have love and support at home.

My husband Blair, no doubt, is the unsung hero of this book. I'm so grateful for all of the times he listened to me, made pots of coffee, fixed my computer, and even tagged along to research institutions when I'm fairly certain he had other things to do.

If not for my close friend and fellow author Audrey Vernick, my research might still be sitting in boxes. Audrey informed me (in the way that only a good friend can) that it was time to stop my never-ending research, turn my hobby into a book, and share it with the world. The idea of writing the book for middle-grade readers (which I had never done) was also Audrey's.

My literary agent at William Morris Endeavor, Mel Berger, was fascinated from the start by the story of Elizabeth Jennings. His enthusiasm and dedication to the project is deeply appreciated. His assistant, David Hinds, kept tabs on the details in a professional manner. My longtime attorney, John R. Firestone, provided professional advice and personal encouragement, as always.

I'm so grateful that *Streetcar to Justice* was published by Greenwillow Books/HarperCollins in New York. A writer could not ask for more. Virginia Duncan, my editor, is a visionary. She instinctively knew that this book would be important not just for young readers but teachers, librarians, and parents. She was passionate about the topic and shared my enthusiasm for history and especially for forgotten stories. Her guidance and support throughout the process were hugely important. She was the perfect editor for me and for this project.

Special thanks to Tim Smith, managing editor at Greenwillow; Paul Zakris, art director; Katie Heit, for helping manage the photos and a thousand other details; Christy Hale, for the challenging job of designing the interior of the book; and Cozbi Cabrera, the brilliant artist who created the cover portrait of Elizabeth Jennings.

I'm not sure I would have tackled this book project had I not written the 1993 oral history *Having Our Say: The Delany Sisters' First 100 Years*. Sarah L. (Sadie) Delany and A. Elizabeth (Bessie) Delany, ages 102 and 100 when I met them, were the daughters of a man born into slavery and a mother who was mixed race but born free. From the Delany sisters I learned black history in depth and firsthand. The sisters, with whom I became close friends, often shared their hopes and expectations for my future career. *Streetcar to Justice* is exactly the type of project I believe they would have wanted me to do. I felt their presence every step of the way.

My father, Lee H. Hill Jr., taught me from a young age to love and appreciate history. Sadly, as I was in the final stretch of finishing this book, he died at the age of 92. For the first time in my life I did not feel like writing. My mother, Dorothy S. Hill, who has always set the standard of professionalism for me, insisted that Dad would have wanted me to keep writing. My three older siblings—Lee H. Hill III, Dr. Jonathan D. Hill, and Helen Hill Kotzky—agreed with Mom and helped me maintain my focus. Members of my writing group, the Sisterhood of Atomic Engineers, grieved with me but kept me laughing, too. I am blessed to have all of you in my life.

Professionals who offered generous assistance include Dr. Prithi Kanakamedala, assistant professor in the history department at Bronx Community College of the City University of New York; Dr. Amy Bass, professor of history and director of the honors program at the College of New Rochelle; John C. Carter and Rita Kline, who provided genealogical-research advice; and Miriam Sicherman, New York City public school teacher extraordinaire.

Part of my job was to find images to go with my written text—the newspaper clippings, photographs, engravings, drawings, and paintings that would help bring the story to life. Among the professionals who provided assistance are Susan K. Forbes, Lisa Keys, and Nancy Sherbert at the Kansas State Historical Society; Eleanor Gillers and Robert Delap at the New-York Historical Society; David Rosado and Andrea Felder at the New York Public Library; Kelly Dyson at the Library of Congress; Rebecca Haggerty at the New York Transit Museum; Alla Roylance at the Brooklyn Public Library—Brooklyn Collection; Erin Beasley at the Smithsonian Institution's National Portrait Gallery; Lauren Robinson at the Museum of the City of New York; and Dana White at the Ossining (New York) Historical Society Museum.

ACKNOWLEDGMENTS

I'd like to think of this book as a testament to the importance of the written word (Elizabeth Jennings's firsthand account of the assault), the free press (which published her letter and related stories), and, of course, the libraries and historical societies which preserved those stories for all time. Without all three, this book could not have been written.

Illustrations

PART I: A Day like No Other

Chapter 1: "Those Monsters in Human Form"

viii, 4: Elizabeth Jennings: Courtesy of Kansas State Historical Society.

6-7: The black middle class: Wood engraving by Theodore R. Davis. Published in *Harper's Weekly*, February 6, 1869. Courtesy of Library of Congress.

8-9: A drawing of New-York (Manhattan) and at right, Brooklyn: John Bachmann (active 1849–1885)/Museum of the City of New York.

10: Crowded and filthy street in Five Points: Robert N. Dennis Collection of Stereoscopic Views, Miriam and Ira D. Wallach Division of Art, Prints and Photographs, The New York Public Library, Astor, Lenox and Tilden Foundations.

11: Five Points 1827, "Intersection of Cross, Anthony and Orange Streets": From *Valentine's Manual*, 1885, page 112, image 35910 (same as image 44668) New-York Historical Society.

13: Tish-Co-Han, a chief of the Lenni-Lenape people: Lithograph circa 1837 by John T. Bowen. Courtesy of Library of Congress.

Chapter 2: Stray Dogs and Pickpockets

14: Both photos from the Lonto/Watson Collection, 1885, Central Crosstown Railroad Cars, 7th Avenue, Manhattan, New York. Courtesy of New York Transit Museum.

16: An advertisement for omnibuses: "All kinds of omnibuses manufactured by John Stephenson, New-York"; wood engraving, advertisement: *Business Encyclopaedia & Commercial Directory*. New York, Emerson, Alvord & Co., 185-?, p. 157; from the Bella C. Landauer Collection scrapbook, image 49100, New-York Historical Society.

17: A horse-drawn streetcar in New York: Photograph by D. Hill, 42nd Street, north side, between 5th and 6th Aves., 1889; from the Geographic File (PR020), box 32, folder: W. 42nd Street—Fifth toward Sixth Avenue, New-York Historical Society.

18: (top) Corner of Pearl and Chatham Streets (now the corner of Pearl Street and Park Row) in 1861: Museum of the City of New York.

18: (bottom) Midsummer in Five Points: Art & Picture Collection, The New York Public Library, Astor, Lenox and Tilden Foundations.

19: "Pork Lively," 1859: Picture Collection, The New York Public Library, Astor, Lenox and Tilden Foundations.

20: A drawing of Five Points in 1859: From *D.T. Valentine's Manual*, 1860 folder, image 74639, New-York Historical Society.

22: Slave Market on Wall Street: Art & Picture Collection, The New York Public Library, Astor, Lenox and Tilden Foundations.

Chapter 3: A City Divided by Race

26: Black chimney sweeps in New York: Photograph taken in 1860s by Charles D. Fredricks. Courtesy of Library of Congress.

32-33: Street map of Manhattan in 1856: Lionel Pincus and Princess Firyal Map Division, The New York Public Library. "Map of the City of New York, 1856 / engrd. for *D.T. Valentine's Manual* 1856 by G. Hayward, 120 Water St., N.Y." New York Public Library Digital Collections

Chapter 4: "I Screamed Murder with All My Voice"

34: Elizabeth Jennings as a young woman. Painting by Cozbi Cabrera.

Chapter 6: An Admired Family

41: Frederick Douglass, 1880: Photo by Mathew B. Brady. The Metropolitan Museum of Art, Gilman Collection, Museum Purchase, 2005.

42: *The Colored American*, September 23, 1837.

44: *The North Star*, published by Frederick Douglass.

45: *Frederick Douglass' Paper*, Sept. 22, 1854.

46: New York African Free School: penmanship with drawing of the exterior of the school; reads "The New York African Free School, erected in the year 1815 . . ."; *Manuscripts Penmanship & Drawing Book*, AFS, 1822, Vol. 4, page 6; c.t. #78742.6, image 59134, New-York Historical Society.

47: A classroom in a school for black children: Colored Orphan Asylum, Good Friday, 1861, interior School Room No. 2 , stereo, image 59133, New-York Historical Society.

Chapter 7: A "Shameful" and "Loathsome" Issue

48: *New-York Daily Tribune*, July 19, 1854.

50: *The Liberator*, May 7, 1831.

51: *New-York Daily Tribune*, September 7, 1850.

53: *New-York Daily Tribune*, September 16, 1850.

56: William Lloyd Garrison: Photographs and Prints Division, Schomburg Center for Research in Black Culture, The New York Public Library, Astor, Lenox and Tilden Foundations.

57: Horace Greeley: Print Collection, Miriam and Ira D. Wallach Division of Art, Prints and Photographs, The New York Public Library, Astor, Lenox and Tilden Foundations.

Chapter 8: A Future U.S. President

58: Chester Arthur in a photograph taken in about 1858: Sixth-plate daguerreotype, National Portrait Gallery, Smithsonian Institution.

61: Capture of a black female fugitive in New York: Manuscripts, Archives and Rare Books Division, Schomburg Center for Research in Black Culture, The New York Public Library, Astor, Lenox and Tilden Foundations.

Chapter 9: *Elizabeth Jennings v. Third Avenue Railroad Company*
64: Brooklyn City Hall (now Borough Hall): Brooklyn Public Library—Brooklyn Collection.

68-69: Crossing from Brooklyn to New-York (Manhattan) across the frozen East River: Brooklyn Public Library—Brooklyn Collection.

Chapter 10: The Jury's Decision
70: A lawyer makes his case: Courtesy of Florida Center for Instructional Technology, College of Education, University of South Florida.

73: Some of the newspapers that published the jury's decision. *The Anti-Slavery Bugle* in Ohio (where editors changed "coloured" to "colored") was one of several newspapers which reprinted the story from the *National Anti-Slavery Standard*.

74-75: Newspaper coverage of the jury's decision: *The Anti-Slavery Bugle*, March 10, 1855, reprinted from the *National Anti-Slavery Standard*, March 3, 1855; *Frederick Douglass' Paper*, March 2, 1855; and *The Brooklyn Daily Eagle*, Feb. 23, 1855. Opposite page, *New-York Daily Tribune,* Feb. 23, 1855, reprinted in *The Pacific Appeal*, May 16, 1863.

PART II: A Forgotten Hero
Chapter 11: An Uncanny Similarity to Rosa Parks
78: Rosa Parks on a bus: Getty Images, Underwood Archives/Contributor.

80: *New-York Daily Tribune*, July 18 and 19, 1854.

Chapter 12: What Happened to Elizabeth Jennings?
84: Burning of the Colored Orphan Asylum during the Draft Riots of 1863: p.12 from "From Cherry Streets to Green Pastures . . .", MSS- Papers of the Association for the Benefit of Colored Orphans, image 74634, New-York Historical Society.

87: Freedman's Bank record: National Archives.

Chapter 13: How a Creepy Old House Led to the Writing of this Book
90: House belonging to Chester Arthur in Ossining, New York: Courtesy of the Ossining Historical Society Museum.

Chapter 14: Retracing Her Footsteps
94: Street sign, Elizabeth Jennings Place: Courtesy of Miriam Sicherman and Michael Rose.

Postscript: Chester A. Arthur: Tragedy Leads to Presidency
100: Chester Arthur being sworn in as President of the United States at his house in Manhattan: Print Collection, Miriam and Ira D. Wallach Division of Art, Prints and Photographs, The New York Public Library, Astor, Lenox and Tilden Foundations.

103: A portrait of Chester Arthur: Portrait painted by Ernest L. Ipsen. Print Collection, Miriam and Ira D. Wallach Division of Art, Prints and Photographs, The New York Public Library, Astor, Lenox and Tilden Foundations.

Index

Abyssinian Baptist Church, 40
activist organizations, 39–40, 76
Adams, John Quincy, 40
Adams, Sarah E., 15, 18–19
    black middle class membership of, 21
    streetcar incident witnessed by, 12, 36,
        37, 67
advertisements
    for omnibuses, 16
    for slaves, *80*, 81
advocacy committee, *48*, 49, 59, 62, 63
African Americans. *See* blacks
African Burial Ground, 22, 97
African Free Schools, 43, *46*
Alger, Horatio, Jr., 21
American Anti-Slavery Society, 55, 56
The Anti-Slavery Bugle, *73*, *74*
Arthur, Chester A.
    in Civil War, 101
    death and, 102
    early years of, 62, 63
    Elizabeth Jennings v. Third Avenue
        Railroad Company and, 59,
        62, 65–66, 71–72, 102
    house of, *90*, 91–92
    images of, 58, 100, 103
    presidency of, *100*, 102
    vice presidency of, 101
Arthur, William, 62, 63

assault of Jennings, E., 36. *See also Elizabeth*
        Jennings v. Third Avenue
        Railroad Company
    written account of, 37–38, *48*, 49, 57,
        67, 83
birth
    of Arthur, C., 62
    of Jennings, E., 113n, 121
    year of, gradual emancipation and, 24
blacks. *See also* segregation; streetcars,
        segregation of
    chimney sweeping, *26*, 27
    disenfranchisement of, 27–28, 115n
    education for, 28, 43, *46*, *47*, 88–89
    equal rights for, 113n
    free, slavery and, 23, 60
    in middle class, 5, *6–7*, 21
    newspapers of, 44, *45*
    opportunity roadblocks for, 21
    peddling, 19–20
boycotts, 55
Bright's disease, 102
Broadway, *19*
Brooklyn, *8–9*
    City Hall of, *64*
Brooklyn Daily Eagle, *73*, *74*
Burrows, Edwin G., 31
Bush, George W., 22

career, 28, 87, 88–89, 119n
Chatham Street (Park Row), *18*, 19, 96, 97, 98
Child, David L., *50*, 52, 55
child labor, 46
Children's Workshop School, 97–98
chimney sweepers, *26*, 27
Chinatown, 97
churches. *See also* First Colored American
        Congregational Church
    Abyssinian Baptist, 40
    of Arthur, W., 62
    segregation in, 29
City Hall, Brooklyn, *64*
civil rights, 113n
    march for, 96
    Parks and, *78*, 79, 81, 82
Civil Rights Act, New York State (1873), 76
civil service, 102
Civil War
    Arthur, C., in, 101
    draft riots of, *84*, 85–86, 87
    Fugitive Slave Act and, 60
    newspapers and, 86
    slavery and, 23, 60, 82
Claudette Colvin: Twice Toward Justice
    (Hoose), 82–83
The Colored American, 1, *42*, 43, 44
Colored Orphan Asylum, *84*
Colvin, Claudette, 82–83
conductors, streetcar
    Jennings, E., assault by, 36, 38–39, *48*, 49,
        57, 67, 83
    Jennings, E., ride refused by, 35
    lawsuit and, 66
    photograph of, *14*, 15
    police officer enlisted by, 37
    segregation role of, 35, 37, *53*, 54
Constitution, U.S.
    Fifteenth Amendment to, 27
    Thirteenth Amendment to, 25, 86
Culver, Erastus D., 59, 62–63
Curtis, Edward, Mrs., 88

Davis, Lewis, *50*, 55
deaths
    Arthur, C., and, 102
    in family, 85, 86, 87, 119n
    of Garfield, 101
    of Jennings, E., 89, 102

de facto segregation, 28
de jure segregation, 28
Delaware Indians, 12, *13*
Democracy in America (Tocqueville), 23
Democratic Party, 101
Dickens, Charles, 11, 43
discrimination, *50*, 52, 55. *See also*
        disenfranchisement; segregation
disease
    Bright's disease, 102
    in New York City, 10
disenfranchisement, 27–28, 115n
doctor, 38
Doherty, Joseph, 96–97, 98
Douglass, Frederick
    black newspapers and, *44*, 45, 72, 73, 74
    Jennings, E., praised by, 40, 45
    Jennings, T. L., and, 39, 40
    photograph of, 40, *41*
    on steamboat discrimination, 52
draft riots, 85–86
    Colored Orphan Asylum burned during, *84*
    Manhattan beginnings of, 87
drivers, streetcar
    Jennings, E., assault by, 36, 38–39, *48*, 49,
        57, 67, 83
    lawsuit and, 66
    photograph of, *14*, 15

East River, 67, *68, 69, 72*
education
    in African Free Schools, 43, *46*
    for blacks, 28, 43, *46*, *47*, 88–89
    career in, 28, 87, 88–89, 119n
    child labor and, 46
    Elizabeth Jennings Place and, 98
    of family, 43, 116n
    for girls, 46, 47
    public, 28, 46
    segregation in, 28
Elizabeth Jennings Place, *94*, 97–98
Elizabeth Jennings v. Third Avenue
    Railroad Company
    Arthur, C., and, 59, 62, 63, 65–66, 71–72,
        102
    filing of, 65–66
    judge in, 67, 69, 71, 72
    jury in, 67, 71
    jury verdict for, 71–72, *73, 74, 75*, 76

researching, 92
streetcar segregation results of, 72, 76
Third Avenue Railroad Company lawyers
    in, 67, 69
trial day for, 66–67, 68, 69
venue for, 64
witnesses testimony in, 67, 117n
emancipation, gradual, 24, 56
Emancipation Proclamation, 23, 86
employment
    of Jennings, E., 28, 87, 88–89, 119n
    segregation and, 26, 27, 28–29
equal rights for blacks, 113n

family, 5, 40, 118n
    deaths in, 85, 86, 87, 119n
    education of, 43, 116n
    Five Points and, 11
    medical assessment ordered by, 38
    trial day travel of, 66–67, 68
Fifteenth Amendment, U.S. Constitution, 27
First Colored American Congregational Church,
        29, 59
    absence from, 5
    advocacy committee of, 48, 49, 59, 62, 63
Five Points
    boundaries of, 113n–114n
    depictions of, 18, 20, 21
    immigrants in, 20
    Jennings, E., steps retraced in, 95–97
    on map, 32, 33
    peddlers in, 19–20
    photograph of, 10
    reputation of, world-wide, 11
Forty-first Street School, 86, 87
Fourth Street, 19
Frederick Douglass' Paper, 44, 45, 72, 73
Freedman's Bank record, 87
Freedom's Journal, 44, 116n
Fröbel, Friedrich, 88, 89
Fugitive Slave Act, 60, 61

Garfield, James A., 101
Garrison, William Lloyd, 56
Geneva Convention, 102
girls, education for, 46, 47
Gotham (Burrows and Wallace), 31
gradual emancipation, 56
    birth year and, 24

Graham, Charles (husband), 85, 86, 87
Graham, Thomas (son), 85
Greeley, Horace, 57. See also New-York Daily
        Tribune

history, forgetting, 79, 98–99
Hoose, Phillip, 82–83
horsecars. See streetcars
hot corn, 18, 20
housing
    of Arthur, C., 90, 91–92
    segregation in, 29–30

immigrants, 29
    in Five Points, 20
internet, research on, 92–93
intersections
    of Broadway and Fourth Street, 19
    of Joseph Doherty, 96–97, 98
    of Pearl and Chatham, 18, 19, 96, 97, 98

Jennings, Elizabeth, viii, 4, 34. See also
        specific topics
Jennings, Elizabeth (mother), 5, 40, 86
    death of, 87
    trial-day travel with, 66–67, 68
Jennings, Thomas L. (father), 5
    activist organization affiliations of, 39–40, 76
    advocacy committee joined by, 49
    death of, 85
    Douglass and, 39, 40
    lawsuit filing and, 65–66
    patent held by, 40
    trial-day travel with, 66–67, 68
Jim Crow, 30, 31
judges, 67, 69, 71, 72
jury
    in Elizabeth Jennings v. Third Avenue
            Railroad Company, 67, 69
    verdict of, 71–72, 73, 74, 75, 76

Kimlau Square, 97
kindergarten, 88–89

landmarks of New York City, 8–9, 68, 113n
    World Trade Center as, 95, 97
lawsuit. See Elizabeth Jennings v. Third
        Avenue Railroad Company
lawyers, 70. See also Arthur, Chester A.
    Culver as, 59, 62–63

of Third Avenue Railroad Company, 67, 69
Legal Rights Association, 76
Lenni-Lenape, 12
chief of, *13*
The Liberator, 55
founder of, *56*
transportation segregation article in, *50*, 52
library, 89
Lincoln, Abraham
Emancipation Proclamation signed by,
23, 86
Greeley and, 57
Lundy, Benjamin, 56

Manhattan, 8–9. *See also* Five Points
African Burial Ground in, 22, 97
Arthur, C., presidential oath in, *100*
draft riot beginnings in, 87
inhabitants of, first, 12, *13*
Jennings, E., steps retraced in, 95–97
map of, 1856, *32–33*
return to, 86–89
segregation in, 29, *51*
streetcars in, 16, *51*
map of Manhattan, 1856, *32–33*
march, civil rights, 96
marriage, 85, 86
medical assessment, 38
memorials, 96–97
middle class, black, 5, *6–7*, 21
minstrel shows, 31
Montgomery, Alabama, *78*, 79
Morse, Herbert, Mrs., 88–89

NAACP. See National Association for the
Advancement of Colored People
National Anti-Slavery Standard, 74
National Association for the Advancement of
Colored People (NAACP), 79, 81
National Colored Convention, *6–7*
National Conventions of Free People of Color, 39
Native Americans, 12, *13*
New England Antislavery Society, 56
New Jersey, 86
newspapers. *See also specific newspapers*
black, *44*, *45*, 72, 73, 74
Civil War and, 86
slavery abolition and, 56–57, *80*, 81
verdict coverage in, 72, *73*, *74*, *75*, 76

New York City. *See also* Manhattan; streets of
New York City
African Free Schools in, 43, *46*
Brooklyn in, *8–9*, *64*
Chinatown in, 97
disease in, 10
drawing of, ca. 1852, *8–9*
Fugitive Slave Act and, 60, 61
inhabitants of, first, 12
kindergarten in, black free, 88–89
landmarks of, 8–9, 68, 95–96, 113n
opportunity roadblocks in, 21
slavery abolished in, 24
streetcars in, *14*, 15, 16, *17*
street filth in, 9, *10*
transportation segregation in, 76
New-York Daily Tribune, 51–52
founder of, *57*
Jennings, E., assault reported by, *48*, 49
slave abolition and, *80*, 81
verdict reported by, 72, *73*, *74*, *75*, 76
New York Slave Market, *22*
New York State
black newspapers in, 44
1873 Civil Rights Act of, 76
Ossining in, *90*, 91–92
slavery abolished in, 23
Supreme Court of, 62, 67
transportation segregation in, 76
The North Star, *44*
Northwest Ordinance, U.S. (1787), 25

omnibuses
advertisements for, *16*
segregation of, *53*, 54
"On the Improvement of the Mind" (Jennings,
E.), *42*, 43
opportunity, roadblocks to, 21
orphan asylum, *84*
Ossining, *90*, 91–92

The Pacific Appeal, *73*, 74, *75*
Park Row. See Chatham Street
Parks, Rosa, *78*
Jennings, E., compared with, 79, 81, 82
patents, 40
Pearl Street, *18*, 19, 96
peddlers, Five Points, 19, 20
Pendleton Act, 102

Philadelphia, 55
Phoenix Society, 40
police
    Jennings, E., encounter with, 37–38
    Jennings, E., steps retraced and, 95–96

racism, 23, 28, 31. *See also*
    disenfranchisement; segregation
Ray, H. Cordelia, 88, 89
recitations, *42*, 43
research, 82, 91–93
Rickard, Leonie G., 88, 89
Rockwell, William, 67, 69, 71, 72

segregation. *See also* streetcars, segregation of
    in churches, 29
    de jure and de facto, 28
    employment and, *26*, 27, 28–29
    in housing, 29–30
    in Manhattan, 29, *51*
    of omnibuses, *53*, 54
    in public education, 28
    of transportation, *50*, 52, 76
sewage, 10
Sicherman, Miriam, 97–98
slavery
    advertising for, *80*, 81
    Civil War and, 23, 60, 82
    free blacks and, 23, 60
    Fugitive Slave Act and, 60
    in New York Slave Market, *22*
    in U.S., northern, *22*, 23–25, *51*, 52–53
slavery, abolition of
    Arthur, C., and, 63
    Arthur, W., and, 62
    newspapers and, 56–57, *80*, 81
    timeline for, 23, 24–25
    transportation segregation and, *50*, *51*
steamboats
    boycotts and, 55
    discrimination on, *50*, 52, 55
Stone, Malvina, 62
streetcars. *See also* conductors, streetcar;
    drivers, streetcar
    in New York City, *14*, 15, 16, 17, 114n
    omnibuses compared with, 16
    tracks for, 97, 114n
streetcars, segregation of. *See also Elizabeth*
    Jennings v. Third Avenue

    Railroad Company
    conductor roles in, 35, 37, *53*, 54
    1850 editorials about, *51*, 52, *53*
    Jennings, E., assault and, 36, 38–39, *48*, 49,
        57, 67, 83
    Jennings, E., police encounter and, 37–38
    Jim Crow and, 30, 31
    slavery and, *51*
streets of New York City. *See also* intersections;
    specific streets
    Elizabeth Jennings Place as, *94*, 97–98
    filth in, 9, *10*
    Jennings, E., steps retraced on, 95–97
    New York Slave Market and, *22*
Supreme Court, New York State, 62, 67

Third Avenue Railroad Company. *See*
    Elizabeth Jennings v. Third
    Avenue Railroad Company
Thirteenth Amendment, U.S. Constitution, 25, 86
Tish-Co-Han, *13*
Tocqueville, Alexis de, 23
tracks, streetcar, 97, 114n
transportation. *See also* streetcars
    omnibus mode of, *16*, 53, 54
    segregation of, *50*, 52, 76
    steamboat mode of, *50*, 52, 55
trolleys. *See* streetcars

Union College, 63
United States (U.S.)
    Constitution of, 25, 27, 86
    northern, slavery in, *22*, 23–25, *51*, 52–53
    northern, transportation segregation in,
        50, 52
    1787 Northwest Ordinance of, 25

Velez-Clarke, Maria, 98
Vermont
    Arthur, C., birth in, 62
    slavery abolished in, 23, 24
voting rights, 27–28, 115n

Wallace, Mike, *31*
Wall Street, *22*
Wilberforce Philanthropic Society, 39
witnesses, 12, 36, 37, 38, 67, 117n
World Trade Center, 95, 97

About the Author

Amy Hill Hearth is a Peabody Award–winning journalist and *New York Times* best-selling author. Her first book, written with the late Sarah L. and A. Elizabeth Delany, was the 1993 oral history *Having Our Say: The Delany Sisters' First 100 Years*. Ms. Hearth, who lives in New Jersey, has long been interested in the history of New York City. Her ancestors arrived in Gravesend, Brooklyn, in 1646. Her ancestry also includes the Native people of New York City, the Lenni-Lenape, sometimes called Delaware Indians. Learn more at www.amyhillhearth.com.